PASSAGE OF TIME

The story
of the Queensferry Passage
and the village of North Queensferry

PETER & CAROL DEAN

ISBN 0-9507858-0-6

PASSAGE OF TIME

Text   Peter Dean

Design and illustration   Carol Dean

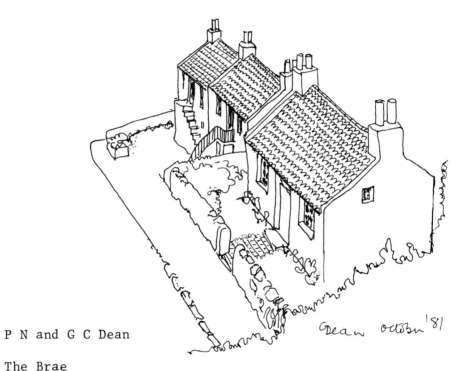

Published by   P N and G C Dean

                    The Brae
                    North Queensferry, Fife
                    Telephone: 0383-414074

Printed by   Watt Chapman Scotland
                    David Watt & Sons Ltd
                    Dunfermline, Fife

Paper supplied by   Inveresk Paper Company Ltd
                    Caldwell's Mill
                    Inverkeithing, Fife

Paper for text   Gemini Matt Cartridge (135 gms)
Board for cover   Gemini Matt Board (260 gms)

Financial support

No undertaking of this nature can be brought to a successful
conclusion without financial support. We have been touched and
impressed by the preparedness of public bodies and businesses
in the area to contribute to a project of special interest to
the local community. We wish to draw readers' attention to the
identity of these concerns in order to acknowledge not only their
important financial contributions but also their community spirit.
We also wish to record our personal thanks for this help.

North Queensferry Community Council
Fife Educational Trust

Dunfermline Building Society, East Port, Dunfermline
Forth Yacht Marina Ltd, North Queensferry
Hewlett-Packard Ltd, South Queensferry
Interscot Heat Treatment Limited, North Queensferry
Inveresk Paper Company Ltd, Caldwell's Mill, Inverkeithing
Bruce Lindsay, The Post Office, North Queensferry
Roxburgh Hotel, North Queensferry
Wm Sanderson & Son Ltd, Scotch Whisky Distillers, South Queensferry
The BP Companies in Scotland

J C Ramage, Licensed Grocer, North Queensferry
J & T Murray, Newsagents, North Queensferry, Dalgety Bay and Inverkeithing

For Alice

Acknowledgements

During the five years we have been working on this project we have
received a great deal of help from a large number of people. We
cannot mention everyone by name but we are nevertheless very grateful
indeed for help, advice, information and encouragement. In particular
we would like to thank Mr and Mrs R A Mitchell of Aberdour for
providing us with the Brock papers; Messrs Torrie and Cooper for the
use of this typewriter; Mrs E P Torrie for advice on the text;
Mr J Oliver and Mrs S Turner for proof-reading; the staffs of the
Dunfermline Library and the National Library of Scotland for their
excellent services; Mr P Crichton, Head of Printing at Heriot-Watt
University for much valuable advice; Mrs S Malcolm for accurate
typing; Mr J Nisbet, ex headmaster, North Queensferry Primary School,
for access to the school log book; Mrs M Oliver for encouragement;
Mr W Martin of the Design Department of Hewlett-Packard Ltd for
specialist advice; Mr W Forrester for marketing information;
the Rev and Mrs T Dennison for invaluable help and Susannah, Catherine
and Josie, our daughters, whose enthusiasm, tolerance and support have
been essential to the completion of this project. For any remaining
errors in the book we have only ourselves to blame.

Peter and Carol Dean
October 1981

PASSAGE OF TIME

Contents

Chapter heading illustrations

Chapter	I	Bronze Age Axe, National Museum of Antiquities of Scotland, Edinburgh
Chapter	II	Burgh Seal of South Queensferry
Chapter	III	Wild Hemlock, Kingscroft, October 1980
Chapter	IV	Eighteenth Century Yawl - contemporary print
Chapter	V	Signal House at Newhalls Pier, South Queensferry
Chapter	VI	Map of Queensferry Passage 1880
Chapter	VII	Herring Creel, Scottish Fisheries Museum, Anstruther
Chapter	VIII	The Brae above the Old School House, North Queensferry
Post Script		Map of Queensferry Passage 1980

Queensferry

For almost a thousand years the Queensferry was the principal ferry
of Scotland. During this time millions of travellers crossed the
Forth here, among them Kings and Queens of Scotland, their nobles,
retinues, armies and thousands of their subjects. Latterly the
motorised traveller joined the cavalcade of history. Many drivers
remember the Queensferry Passage with affection. Today, as they
speed past, travellers glance down on the small communities on each
side of the water. Beneath the majestic sweep of the bridges they
spy piers stretching out into the stream as if to grasp some long
since departed ferry boat, and at the water's edge they see a
jumble of cottages celebrating an era before the advent of town
planning. Here the past vies with the present, evoking journeys
made long ago. The following pages tell the story of the
Queensferry Passage and of North Queensferry tracing the patterns
made upon them by the passage of time.

CHAPTER I

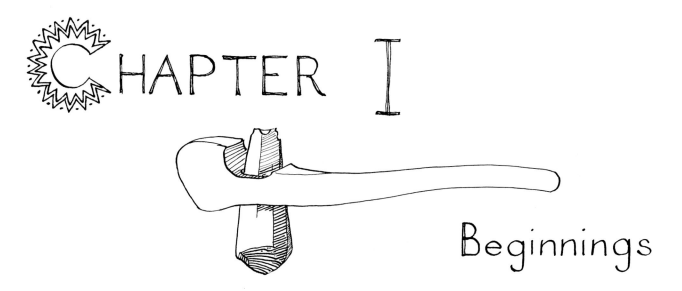

Beginnings

Over 900 years ago, a Saxon princess named Margaret arrived in the Forth estuary. She is reputed to have landed close to North Queensferry. Later this place was named St Margaret's Hope, for she was to become both Queen of Scotland and a Saint of the Catholic Church. Later too, the ferry crossing here, which she is thought to have founded, was also named after her and so too were the villages on each side of the river.

Long before Queen Margaret however, these parts were inhabited. Before its present name, North Queensferry was known as Caschilis ("narrow Firth") or Ardehinnechenan, being impossible to translate, but referring to a high headland. We know almost nothing of the early inhabitants, because they left no written record and very little else besides. We imagine they may have been fishermen, even early ferrymen. The discovery of a dug-out canoe under the sands of Port Laing supports this idea, but the remains were never accurately identified and have long since disappeared. Another 19th century discovery, however, has survived: a small earthenware urn about the size of a teacup containing the ashes of human bones. The discovery was made in March 1859 in the grounds of Craig Dhu. Here on a knoll, close to the water's edge, a cairn of stones had been built, 40-50 feet in diameter. Under this were found three graves dating from 1500-2000 years BC. What a commotion this discovery caused! The owner of the property held a large tea party and invited two eminent archeologists from Edinburgh to address the assembled throng. The guests turned up prepared to be uplifted and informed; the archeologists did not.

Of the 2500-3000 year period between these early settlers and the arrival of Queen Margaret, almost nothing is known. We believe that the level of the Forth was much higher at this period. The local evidence for this is the raised beach behind Port Laing which marks the previous level of the water; the sand and shells found from time to time in excavation works in the low-lying parts of the old village; and the discovery of whale bones under one of the cottages there in the 19th century. This suggests that the land now occupied by the oldest part of the village may then have been under water, and that the peninsula was an island. For these reasons it is quite plausible that prehistoric inhabitants would have used boats.

We can guess with reasonable confidence that the Romans landed here because, for several hundred years, the opposite shore of the Forth formed the Northern boundary of the Roman Empire. The Roman lines of communication ran East-West between Inveresk, Cramond and Bridgeness. The first two were Roman camps, the latter, the beginning of the Antonine Turf wall. In order to defend this line stretching between the Forth (Bodotria) and Clyde (Clota), supplies to feed and equip an estimated 20-30,000 men had to be brought from the South. They would have been most conveniently carried by sea. It therefore seems realistic to suppose that Roman galleys were as common a sight then as freighters bound for Grangemouth are today.

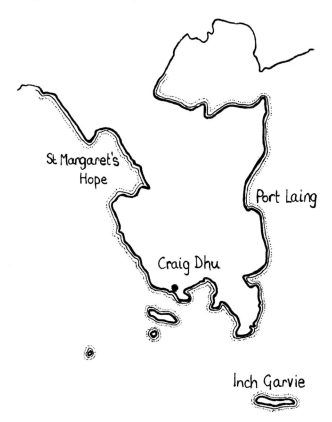

At this time North Queensferry would have been the Southern most tip of the Pictish kingdom. North Queensferry, separated as it is by only 1¼ miles of water from the southern shore, would have been a convenient crossing place for the

Roman legionnaries on diplomatic, exploratory
or punitive expeditions into Fife.   But when
in the period 80-85 AD Agricola decided to
suppress the Caledonii, he appears to have
decided to cross the river much higher up, near
Stirling.   Very little of Roman origin has been
found in Fife, and there is no clear evidence
of Roman occupation.   At North Queensferry
we have a putative Roman way traversing the
hillside above Inchcolm Drive, in an East-West
direction, to end up near the point where a
plaque commemorates the opening of the Road
Bridge by Queen Elizabeth II in 1964.   The
old road to Inverkeithing over the Ferryhills
has also been termed a Roman road, but its many
turns and corners (now no longer enjoyed because
of quarry workings) point to a native origin.

Following the Romans, the Angliae invaded the
Kingdom of Northumbria which stretched right up
to the southern banks of the Forth and had Edinburgh
as its northern stronghold.   A report of the many
conflicts between the Picts and Angliae suggests
that contemporary travellers went via what later
became known as the Queensferry passage.   In the
8th century, King Hungus, a leader of the Picts
invaded Northumbria inflicting a humiliating
defeat on the Angliae under King Athelstane, at
the place in Lothian now known as Athelstaneford.
Fordun narrates that after the battle King Hungus
set Athelstane's head on a pike and placed it on
Inch Garvie mid-way between North and South
Queensferry.   Such a gesture would have been
futile if there had not been travellers passing to
witness the spectacle.

Later, the banks and islands of the Forth became
a veritable magnet for self-supporting communities
of Culdee missionaries.   When the Danes came, these
missionaries were first in the firing line.   Thus
when in 870 AD King Humber and his brother Hubbai
invaded Fife, they slew an estimated 6,000 people
including St Adrian and St Monance.   The latter
is still commemorated in the name of one of the
East Neuk fishing villages.   In 1034 AD the
kingdom was invaded by another large Danish force
lead by Sueno the Great, King of Denmark.   It
sailed up the Forth past Queensferry to land at
Culross, forcing the Scots army under Duncan to
retreat to Perth.   There the Danes would have won
a resounding victory, but for the unsportsmanlike
activities of Duncan: having surrendered
unconditionally, he laced the victors' wine with
belladonna.   Happily, for the Scots, this
poisoned most of the Danish soldiers.   The following
year the Danes mounted a punitive expedition.   The
force, presumably composed of more careful

drinkers, landed at Kinghorn only to be defeated by
Banquo and Macbeth whose victory is recorded in
Shakespeare's lines:

> "Sweno the Norway's King craves composition
> Nor would we deign him burial of his men
> Till he disbursed at Saint Colm's Inch
> Ten thousand dollars to our general use."

We do not know whether the Queensferry peninsula
was inhabited in these violent times.   It would
certainly have proved an excellent look-out post
to give warning of sea-borne invaders.   From the
top of Ferryhills one can see 30 miles down river
to the sea, and 30 miles or more inland to the
distant mountains of the Scottish heartlands.
Few more suitable places exist for lighting
beacons to give early warning of sea invaders to
those dwelling further inland.   Furthermore a
chance of nature provides a fresh water loch at
this high point.

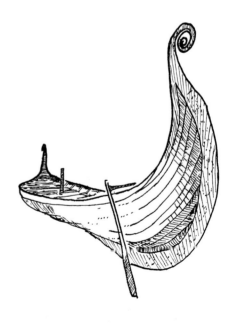

Viking Long Boat

Queen Margaret

After so many years it is difficult to distinguish the myths concerning Queen Margaret, from the facts. Certainly she was a Saxon princess and her brother, Edgar Atheling, had a claim to the English throne. He was therefore a marked man after the Battle of Hastings when the Normans established themselves in power. In 1067 he organised a revolt at York which resulted in the death of 3,000 Normans. Later he was aided by the King of Scotland, Malcolm Canmore (literally meaning "Malcolm, big head"), but Norman reinforcements arrived from the South, and these proved too strong an opposition. In October 1069 Edgar, Margaret, and their sister Christina accompanied by other Saxons, set sail from Monks Wearmouth in Northumbria. Tradition has it that they were heading for Hungary, the birthplace of their mother, but that a storm drove them into the Firth of Forth. In view of the fact that the eligible, widowed, Malcolm Canmore was already friend and ally, it seems plausible to suppose that they had always intended to sail for Scotland. If correct, this theory destroys some of the romance of the shipwrecked princess being rescued by the gallant King, but it is still consistent with a storm in the Firth of Forth, which landed them at Queensferry rather than any other point on the east coast of Scotland. Even so, a landing so convenient for the Scottish capital at Dunfermline seems unlikely to have occurred by chance.

Since childhood Margaret had been destined for a religious life but soon after her arrival in Scotland she and Malcolm were married. She seems to have been an energetic, scholarly and cultured woman with interests in architecture and medicine besides in administrative and church affairs. Turgot, her biographer, and also her confessor, suggests that she had a profoundly civilising effect on the Court and on Scottish society. This has been the verdict of later generations.

The Lothians had come under Scottish rule following the Battle of Carham in 1018 and Malcolm decided to improve the defences of his enlarged kingdom by strengthening the castle at Edinburgh. This meant that he had to cross the Forth frequently to supervise the works, doubtless often accompanied by Margaret. Her chapel still stands on the castle rock, built in a Norman style similar to that of Dalmeny Church and the nave of Dunfermline Abbey. On the Hawes Brae above South Queensferry a large cross was erected and here Queen Margaret is reputed to have encouraged needy people to come to her for help. Turgot relates that "as the religious devotion of the people brought many from all the parts of the church to St Andrews, she constructed dwellings on both sides of the Firth of Forth in order that the poor might find refreshment and lodgings on their way thither and she also provided free ferry boats".

Margaret's final journey to Dunfermline was as dramatic as her first. She died at Edinburgh shortly after hearing of the death of her husband and son. The castle rock was surrounded by enemies. In order to take her remains for burial in Dunfermline, her body was smuggled out of the castle. Her bearers reached the safety of the North shore of the Forth because they were enveloped in a thick mist. This is said to have appeared miraculously on their leaving Edinburgh, and only lifted when they were safe from pursuit. Margaret died at the age of 46, the mother of 8 children, three of whom were destined to be kings of Scotland.

Queen Margaret died in 1093 but the first mention of "Queensferry" by something like its modern name was over 70 years later. In 1164 Malcolm IV granted to the Abbot and monks of Scone a free passage "ad portam reginae", which literally means to the gate or port of the Queen. This refers not to the ferry passage, but to the town of South Queensferry, which has always been the larger of the two Queensferries. Thus by this charter, monks of Scone coming south to Edinburgh would have free passage over the Forth. The earliest reference to the ferry passage is in a charter of David I, who, in 1129 or 1130, granted "the passage and ship of Inverkeithing as I have it in my lordship" to the Abbey of Dunfermline, "on condition that all travellers and messengers coming to and from me and also the persons belonging to my court and also my sons, have free passage in the same ship". This grant was typical of the man whose piety and generosity towards the church were celebrated in Wintoun's lines

> "He illumined in his days
> His lands with kirks and with abbays."

James I, looking at his predecessor's generosity from a different point of view, remarked ruefully that David I was a "sair sanct for the croun".

The grant of David I was confirmed by Pope Alexander in 1163, in a charter which refers to "half (dimidium) of the passage of Inverkeithin", suggesting that at this time the Abbey of Dunfermline owned only half of the ferry passage. This is supported by a reference in 1158 to the Abbot of Dunfermline and a certain Gospatrick as "Lords of the ferries".

Greyfriars' Hospitium, Inverkeithing

We have seen that so far no specific reference to North Queensferry has been made; indeed the earliest references link the ferry passage with Inverkeithing. This raises an interesting question: was the North end of the passage located at this time at Inverkeithing? The phrase "the Passage and ship of Inverkeithing" appears to support this theory. Moreover, in 1211 when Innocent III confirmed the right of Dunfermline Abbey to what was now termed the Queensferry passage (Passagium Regina), he also confirmed the

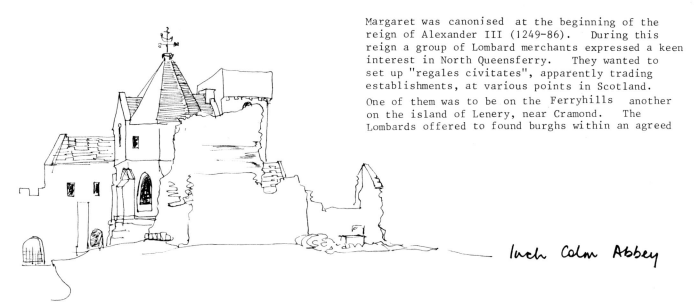

Inch Colm Abbey

Margaret was canonised at the beginning of the reign of Alexander III (1249-86). During this reign a group of Lombard merchants expressed a keen interest in North Queensferry. They wanted to set up "regales civitates", apparently trading establishments, at various points in Scotland.

One of them was to be on the Ferryhills another on the island of Lenery, near Cramond. The Lombards offered to found burghs within an agreed

Abbey's ownership "beside Inverkeithing of certain land that is called the land of the hostel". This would seem to be a reference to the hostel set up by Queen Margaret at the North end of the ferry. There is no local tradition of a mediaeval hospitium at North Queensferry, although to be fair, St James Chapel could be the ruins of one. One of the oldest parts of Inverkeithing is known as Spittalfields, literally meaning the lands of the hostel. Finally, to have continued the river crossing to Inverkeithing would have been a method of avoiding transhipment of goods and the relatively difficult land journey over the Ferryhills , without greatly increasing the cost or the danger of the water journey.

Irrespective of whether the ferry passage terminated here or further north, the spirit of Queen Margaret remained. In 1123, her son, Alexander I, was crossing the Forth here, when a storm blew up and ship-wrecked him on Inch Colm. There he lived with a culdee hermit for several days, on a less than kingly diet. How he left the island is not known but once back on the mainland, he decided to found a monastery on Inch Colm in gratitude for his safe delivery. Another episode is reminiscent of Margaret's own final journey to Dunfermline. In 1153, David I, another of her sons, died at Carlisle. His body was to be returned to Dunfermline, but on reaching the southern shore of the Forth, the cortege halted because of a dangerous storm. Once in the passage boat however, the storm subsided and the waters remained calm throughout the crossing. When the travellers reached the northern shore, however, the storm resumed in all its fury.

In 1246 the Pope appointed a commission to enquire into the life and miracles of Queen Margaret, and in 1249 or 1250 she was canonised. Forty years after this Pope Nicholas IV granted relaxation of a year and forty days penance to penitents who visited her shrine at Dunfermline upon her festival (19th June). Consequently, by the 13th century the Queensferry Passage was beginning to live up to its name. Confusingly, however, well before Margaret's canonisation, charters relating to the Queensferry Passage (in 1184 and 1234) refer to her as Saint Margaret, the Queen. So perhaps in 1250 the Pope was giving formal recognition of saintly qualities, already widely recognised.

period of years in return for freedom of worship. From the 13th century onwards, the Lombards, originally from Northern Italy, flourished as money lenders, bankers, and merchants in London. In fact the three golden balls of the pawnbroker are said to have derived through them from the armorial bearings of the Medici family of Florence. In any event, Alexander refused their application. Barbieri, a 19th century historian of Fife, and himself an Italian comments on Alexander's refusal: "wealthy Jews .... a new Jerusalem, an emporium of commerce, a city of refuge, a rallying point for their wandering nation .... As usual bigotry and jealousy gave the death blow to this laudable design". By the same token the village of North Queensferry narrowly missed becoming a burgh.

Inch Colm Abbey weather vane

Of greater interest, perhaps, is the grant, in 1275, by Abbot Ralph of Dunfermline, of 8 oars in the new passage boat ("Carta de VIIj remis batello passagii" Register of Dunfermline No 320). The grant is by Ralph de Greenlaw, Lord Abbot of Dunfermline to 7 persons:

    John Armiger
    Peter, the son of Adam
    Thomas, the son of Bernard
    Richard de Kirkeland
    Magote de Craggy
    John Flocker
    Eue, daughter of John Harloth

The charter is a deed of sasine conferring what

is presumably a leasehold interest on these seven people. Each received one oar, representing a one eighth interest in the ferry boat, except John Armiger who receives two, which will pass to his "heirs and assignees excepting ecclesiastics". These two oars are to be supervised by Susanne, wife of the same John, during the whole of her life and she is to account to the abbey yearly. The annual rent is fixed at eight pence for each oar, payable, half at Martinmas and half at Pentecost. In addition, those granted oars are to continue to pay the old ferry rent and to provide services to the abbot according to longstanding custom. It seems unlikely that Susanne, wife of John Armiger, or Eue, daughter of John Harloth, actually pulled the oars. They must have employed others to do so. Magote de Craggy sounds like a woman also. The local name for rock is craig, and her surname may well indicate where she lived, just as Richard de Kirkeland's may do.

Monarchs have crossed the Queensferry Passage, both alive and dead. In 1286 Alexander III crossed on a stormy night to ride to his death a few hours later at Kinghorn. The night was allegedly dark and stormy. Arriving at Queensferry, the ferry master advised him to go back. Having ignored this warning he was invited by the master of his salt works at Inverkeithing to spend the night there before continuing the journey, an invitation he had accepted on previous occasions. He once more refused and between Burntisland and Kinghorn he was thrown from his horse and killed. His death may not have been completely accidental. One story is that he was warned by a seer that his death would be caused by his horse. Accordingly to prevent the prophesy from being realised, he had the horse killed, but did not know that its bones lay on the sands at Kinghorn. On the fatal night his mount caught sight of the bones, reared, and threw him to his death. Alternatively and more prosaically, he may have been murdered by his attendants.

Another colourful episode but this time with firmer evidence and a happier ending occurred in 1342 during the Abbacy of Alexander. By this time the Abbey of Dunfermline owned both halves of the Queensferry Passage, together with lands on either side of the river. As well as their rights of ownership, the Abbey had a customary right to the landing places on either side of the passage. The Abbot's landing place on the south side was west of the present harbour at a rock called "The Binks". The Abbot claimed a right to this since time immemorial. (An imprint of Queen Margaret's foot was believed to be visible upon this rock's surface, and was a source of reverence among the ferrymen.) James de Dundas impudently chose this rock for landing cargoes, and continued to do so despite warnings from the Abbot. Finally the Abbot resorted to the ultimate deterrent: excommunication. James de Dundas apparently valued his spiritual welfare more than his cargoes. Accordingly he appeared on South Queensferry shore before the assembled inhabitants. The Abbot and his entourage appeared, and exhibited the confirmations of their proprietorial rights to the Ferry Passage from David I, through the various intermediate kings and Popes down to 1342. Dundas humbly supplicated the Abbot for forgiveness, who then absolved him of excommunication "but were molestation ever to be repeated he should immediately incur the same censure".

St. James' chapel

We have just said that by the middle of the 14th century Dunfermline Abbey owned both halves of the Queensferry Passage. Shortly after Bannockburn Robert the Bruce made three gifts to Dunfermline Abbey: North Queensferry Chapel; "Half of the passage of the Queen that Roger de Mowbray possessed;" and "the ferry field near Inverkeithing with the new great custom, as also 5 merks yearly out of the revenues of the Burgh of Inverkeithing". Roger de Mowbray's property had been forfeit for his part in opposing Bruce and represented part of the spoils of war: his loss was the Abbey's gain. The grant of North Queensferry Chapel, which incidentally is not termed a hospitium, represents the first specific mention of this village by name. The ruins of this Chapel still stand in the centre of the old village, east of the main street. The wording of the grant implies that the Chapel was already an ancient foundation because it refers to "pertinents belonging to it by right or antiquity". The Chapel, whenever founded, was dedicated to St James, patron saint of travellers, a dedication highly appropriate for a village through which large numbers of travellers passed. Travellers commencing

St. James' Chapel, North Queensferry

journeys could pray here for a safe journey while those completing them could thank God for a safe return. It seems hardly a coincidence that Kinghorn, another old ferry village should also have a chapel of St James.

Robert the Bruce's gift was made for the safety of his own soul and those of his ancestors and successors. It had several conditions:

1. the monks and their successors were to provide two chaplains to celebrate divine service in the Chapel for all time

2. they were to repair the Chapel and keep it up at their own expense

3. they were to provide it with a chalice, vestments, books and other useful and necessary ornaments.

In 1323 William, Bishop of St Andrews, confirmed this charter. In the same year King Robert issued an order at Dundee to the magistrates of Inverkeithing who appear to have been tardy in paying the 5 merks which Bruce had granted out of their revenue, to Dunfermline Abbey. This grant was confirmed over 100 years later by James II.

The next reference to the Chapel is some 150 years after Bruce's grant. Even in that relatively short time the chaplains appointed to celebrate divine service for all time had ceased operation. This is evident from a grant of December 1479 by Henry Creighton, Abbot of Dunfermline, who bestowed upon "our beloved chaplain Sir David Story the office of chaplain founded anew by us in the Chapel of St James the apostle in North ferry". By a curious coincidence in the previous year, certain Kinghorn lands were granted for the support of the new hostel and for the maintenance of a chaplain in that Chapel of St James. The need to appoint a new chaplain at North Queensferry may have arisen because of pluralism or absenteeism. Thus Sir David Story was required to "reside continually at and dwell in the manse of the Chapel" and was warned that should he undertake any other cure or involve himself in any other office or have his residence elsewhere thus causing the services to suffer neglect, the chaplaincy was to pass to the Abbot and be declared vacant. The chaplaincy moreover was to remain in the patronage of the Abbot. Despite these restrictions, Sir David seems to have had quite a good bargain. The emoluments were a salary of 10 merks Scots annually, a manse and garden situated near the Chapel, 2 acres of low-lying land on the Ferryhills and pasture for a horse, and, with a few exceptions, offerings made at the altar. In addition he was to receive each year 20 francs Scots from two tenements in Dunfermline for upholding the ornaments and vestments of the altar. All in all, Sir David would have been able to afford a style of life quite different from that enjoyed by many of his parishioners,

The tradition of gentleman clerics seems to have died hard at North Queensferry. In 1533 we find Sir John Brown (now termed vicar, not chaplain) in dispute with one Nicoll Thomson who had apparently settled on the Kirklands and had been in peaceful possession of them for four or five years. The Regality Court of Dunfermline confirmed the latter's tenure until he was given just notice to quit. What sort of man this Nicoll Thomson was, is unclear, but 20 years later he is accused of drowning three oxen belonging to David Anderson.

James IV

Let us turn to James IV, that most congenial of Scottish monarchs, who in 1507 came to make offerings to his namesake at the Chapel in North Queensferry. The Lord High Treasurer's accounts reveal him to be a generous giver both to churches and to the poor, so the offerings he made here were in no way unusual. It is best to bear in mind that at this time "Queensferry" is sometimes used as an omnibus term meaning both North and South Queensferry: more frequently however, it implies South Queensferry. North Queensferry is referred to as North Ferry, with Ferry variously spelled as ferye, ferre, etc. In the following quotations fraucht means fare (modern English: freight), feryaris means the ferrymen and the final 'j' in the numbers simply signifies the final digit so xviijS is 18/- and iiijd is 4 pence.

1496	Item to the man of the Fery that sellis sclatis in erlis for sclatis (1)	xviij s
1497	Item the IX day of Julij the King passit to Kingorne giffin to the botemen of the Quenisfery	xiiij s
	Item to the lycht in the kirk of the Quenisfery	xiiij s
	Item (the X day of Julij) to the pur folk in Kingorne	iiij x
1504	Item the XV day of Januar the King passit to Faulkland to the Feryaris at the Quenisfery	xxviij s
	Item that nicht to the King to play at the tables with Robert Colville in Faulkland	xxviij s
	Item to the Feryaris of the Quenisfery for the fraught of divers botis with the court	iij Franch crounis
	Item the xxij day of September payit to Johne Bertoun he laid down to the Feryaris of the Quenis Ferye quhen the King passit to Dunfermlyn	xlij s
	Item payit to the Abbot of Cambuskinneth he gaif to the botemen of the Quenis Fery the ferd day of October that had the King ouer the water divers botis	
	Item that he gaf to the Feryaris at the Quenis ferye the vij day of October the King cummand to Dunfrmlym	xxj s iiij d

Item to the botis of the
Quenis Ferye that brought
the King and Quene fra the
Quenis Fery to the New Havin
and for bred and aill in the
samyn boats

Item for the Quenis hors
fraucht at the Fery   xxxj s

Item for hors to the More
lasses (2) and for cariage
hors to the bestis to the
Quenis Fery and syne to
Inverkethin and for thair
fraught to the Fery   x s viij d

Item the xxvij day of
November to the Kingis
offerand in Sanct James
Chapell of the North
Ferye   xiij s

1507   Item to the Kingis offerand
       in Sanct James Chapell of
       the Quenis Ferye   xiiij s

(1)   sclatis = slates; in erlis for = in earnest
                                                for

(2)   horses for the moorish lasses, apparently
      dancers

The Naval exploits of James IV deserve particular
mention because his flag ship, "The Great Michael"
was once moored opposite the village. At least,
this is a pretext for recounting a splendid
episode concerning his Admiral, Sir Andrew Wood
of Largo, which is not strictly relevant to our
local history.   In 1488 Sir Andrew Wood with
"Mayflower" and "Yellow Carvel", two
converted merchant vessels, intercepted and
captured 5 English fighting ships which he
brought back to Leith.   Henry VII of England,
infuriated by such impudence, mounted a punitive
expedition under Sir Stevin Bull, to bring
back Sir Andrew Wood of Largo "quick or dead".
His three ships sailed up the East coast to the
Forth Estuary.   At the back of the May Island
beyond the Bass Rock, they were sighted by
Sir Andrew Wood, in charge of two smaller
Scottish ships.   "Then the captane was verrie
blyth and gart fill the wyne and drink about
to all the skipperis and captanes that was
under him".   Sir Andrew Wood came forth
"knowing no impediment of enemies to be in his
gait" and advised his crews to make ready "Bot
above all use the fireballis weill in the topis
of the schipes" .... "so he caused perce the
wyne and everie man drank to other".   No doubt
they needed Dutch courage because the fight
lasted the whole day and with the coming of
darkness "night severed thame".   The next
morning battle was rejoined and the ships
entered the mouth of the Tay.   "The Scottismen
siend this they tuik sick courage and hardiment
that they doubled on the strokis of the
Inglismen, and thair tuik Stevin Bull and his
thrie shipes and had thame up to the towne of
Dundie".   James IV thanked Sir Andrew on his
return and gave him rich gifts.   Sir Stevin
Bull and his men he sent back with gifts to
the King of England "to let him understand
that he had also manlie men in Scotland as he
had in Ingland; thair foir desired him to send
no more of his captanes in tyme cuming".

Other boats in James IV's navy were: James,
Margaret, Treasurer, Pansy, Lark and Christopher.
There was even a contemporary ship (possibly a
fast runner) known as "Merry Buttocks".

A few years later James IV conceived a grandiose
plan for an unprecedentedly large, purpose-built
warship.   The result was the "Great Michael"
built and launched at New Haven in 1511.
This 16th century equivalent of the Concorde
airliner, was 240 feet long, had sides 10 feet
thick, and cost £30,000 to build, not counting
armaments.   She was armed to the teeth with
six big guns on each side, two at the stern, and
one at the bow, besides pieces of small artillery
including "falcons, slings, serpentines,
hackbutts, and crossbows".   The complement was
120 gunners and 300 sailors and the wage bill
£126 per week.   At its launching 3 trumpeters
and a drummer received 17 shillings for their
part in the ceremony and rather characteristically
James IV had a cannon fired at his ship to test
its strength (with no deleterious effect).

The Great Michael

For a voyage of unknown length the "Great Michael"
was provisioned as follows:

  289 barrels of ale

  174 barrels of beer

   29 tuns of wine

    1 barrel of pellock (probably salt porpoise)

   6½ chalders of oatmeal

  200 salt marts (herring)

   40 fresh marts

   40 salt pork

1,000 corf keling (dried cod)

5,300 stock fish

   13 barrels of salmon

    5 lasts of herring

  600 eggs

  916 cheeses (equivalent to 200 stone)

   42 stone of butter

      and a large quantity of biscuits

In 1512 the "Great Michael" was brought up to the Queensferry. While moored here, the King paid frequent visits to his new toy. Here are some of the extracts from the Lord High Treasurer's Accounts:

1512   Item to Robert Jameson of the Quenis Fery for tuelf pece of grete and small tymmer

Item to Maister Thomas Diksone to by fische and uthir stuff to have up to the Kingis gret schip in the Quenisferry

Item to Johnesone of Ferre to seik the depis and passage to the Pollertht

Item the last day of Junij to the botismen at rowit the King to the great schip and syne to the Quenis Ferry

Item gewin be Wille Wod for Thomson's boit of the Quenis Ferry at had the King up to the great schip

Item to botismen at brocht the Quenis bedis and coferris oure the watter

Item to ane botisman of the Quenis Ferry for careing of tymmer to the gret schip diverse tymez

Item to Sande Makcullocht for collationis to the King in the Quenis ferry

Item in Johnesonis hous of the Fery for grathing of the sam fische to the Kingis dennar

Item to ane fidlair thair

1513   Item payt to Schir Johne Ramsay quilk he layd done to the marynaris that past with the Queen fra the Blackness to the Quenis Ferry

Item fra Ramsay the Baxtar of the ferry, a pype and a puncion of aile

Item resavit fra Wille Ramsay of the ferry quheit breid bocht be me.

The story of the Battle of Flodden has been told elsewhere. At this battle James IV in an unnecessary gesture of bravery led the Scottish army into battle. The result was a crushing defeat, in which Scotland lost her King, 12 earls, 14 lords, and perhaps 10,000 men. From a strictly local point of view we could also say that Queensferry lost a good friend.

After Flodden

Following the death of James IV references to Queensferry dwindle. Despite this neglect the ferrymen appear to have been alive and well. In October 1523, James V sent Andrew Dishington with a letter charging the ferrymen of Leith, Kinghorn and Queensferry that "na boit may rais ony fraucht on the peipill bot the auld fraucht

under the pane of deid". The penalty seems disproportionately severe in relation to the offence, but perhaps it was intended mostly as a deterrent. Communications were poor; the central authority weak, so that it was difficult to prevent the ferrymen exploiting their local monopoly . At the rates set down by Parliament, their means of livelihood were slender so it was natural for them to raise the charges to what the traffic would bear.

The earliest Act of Parliament concerning Ferries was in 1425 when James I ordained that all Ferries where horse were ferried, should have a "treyn brig" (gang plank) for each boat so that the travellers' horses could be received on board without hurt. The penalty for non compliance was 40 shillings for each boat. It seems likely that the statute did not accomplish its ends because a similar act was passed in 1467 "for the utility and profit of the King's highness and his lieges who diverse times pass over ferries with their horses". The Act mentioned all of Scotland's main ferries including Kinghorn, Leith and Queensferry, and ordered that bridges be made within 20 days for the ease of shipping horses. The penalty was confiscation of the boat, besides being banned from ferrying for ever and a day. Virtually the same Act was passed in 1469 when it was acknowledged that the ferrymen concerned had been negligent in heeding the previous legislation. In 1474, the rules concerning the building of "bridges" were repeated, but this time the charges were regulated too. At Kinghorn a man or a woman was to cross for two pence, and "for the horse, burden and person there shall be paid but sixpence". "And at Quenisferry shall be taken but one pence of the man, and of the horse two pence and all in the form and manner above written". Ferrymen disregarding the 1474 Act were to pay 40 shillings to the King. Nor was this Act much observed, because four years later yet another Act confirmed that "it is statute and ordained that in time to come no ferrier take more fraucht of the horse, man, nor goods but famekle (as much) as is statute .... under the pain of £5 to be paid to our sovereign lord .... and this to be a point of dittay (indictment) in time to come".

We can now see in its proper perspective the threat to execute any ferryman who exceeded the statutory charges. It was a desperate threat against determined and persistent law breakers. As the story of Queensferry unfolds we shall see that the ferrymen enjoyed a long period of untrammelled independence, during which they ruled the roost, by turns bullying their passengers or cajoling them, overcharging them or abusing them, ever the subject of official proclamations trying to limit their activities, but seldom if ever heeding them, however dire the penalties. Only several centuries later when the exigencies of national economic development demanded it, were these unruly men finally forced into unwilling conformity, and then only by breaking their grip on the working of the ferry passage. For the moment their grip remained as tight as ever. Another letter was delivered by Andrew Dishington in 1523 which was the prototype down the centuries for numerous others; "ane lettre to be execute and proclamit in Leith and Quenis Ferre that na northt land men returne oure the watter to the agane cumming of my lord governor fra the camp under pane of deid". Clearly the intention is to prevent the Northmen from returning home, presumably because they were needed for military purposes. If the ferries could be stopped or their services denied, the Forth would constitute a natural barrier. Thus when the authorities wished to prevent their allies retreating, their enemies advancing, or the plague from spreading, a first step would be to close the Queensferry. The general needs of national security, however, were contrary to the particular economic needs of the Ferrymen, so that while closing the Queensferry was often a wise strategic move, it was often difficult to achieve in practice.

In June 1538, James V married Mary of Guise Lorraine in St Andrews Cathedral. She landed at Fifeness in ships sent by the King and manned by volunteer mariners from the Forth ports. In July 1538 the new Queen made a royal progress through Fife from St Andrews to Queensferry, finally making a triumphal entry into Edinburgh via the West Port (near today's Salvation Army Hostel in the Grassmarket). In the final stages of her progress the ferrymen of hereabouts played a modest but necessary part:

> Item to John Bertane for grathing of
> the Kingis row boit in tymmer
> werkmanschip, salis and pantyne of
> hir salis and to the childers wages
> and to the ferry boit that past all to
> the Quenis Ferry to bring oure the
> quenis grace at hir entres in
> Edinburgh"   £9-8-6d

She was followed by horses, furniture and other accoutrements:

> "The kingis tapescherie and utheris his
> geir were transported of Sanctadrois
> to Edinburghe"

> "Item for carying of the Dames of Honouris
> beddis fra Dunfermline to
> Edinburgh   3 shillings

Only five years separate James V's second marriage from his death. In late November 1542 an invading English army, despatched by the warlike Henry VIII, defeated a Scottish army at Solway Moss. A few days later a distraught James took to his bed at Falkland Palace. On the 8th December, 1542, the birth of a daughter (later to be Mary Queen of Scots) was announced, which seems to have deepened his melancholy. He gave up the ghost in mid December. An entry in the Lord High Treasurer's Account of New Years Day 1543 closes this section "Gevin to twa boyis passand witht diligence to warne the gentill men in Fyffe for conveying the Kingis grace body fra Falkland to the Ferry"   16 shillings.

Versions of the Ship of Inverkeithing: Town House; Burgh Seal; School House

CHAPTER II

Troubled Times

With the death of James V we enter a time of trouble, the ripples of which spread from the centre to North Queensferry and far beyond. On top of religious contention, heightened since James V's marriage with the Roman Catholic Mary of Guise, there came an invasion from the South. The resultant war which ebbed and flowed leaving different parts of the Forth Estuary at different times in enemy hands forms a confusing and dangerous background to our local story. It started in 1544 with Hertford at the head of an English army, burning Edinburgh, Leith and Holyrood besides 7 monasteries and 240 villages. One feature of the months which preceded the Scottish defeat at Solway Moss was the freedom with which the English navy moved in the Firth of Forth. The Scottish navy was bottled up in St Margaret's Hope, allowing the English Navy to make coastal attacks, for instance at Aberdour, which was burned. While protracted battle campaigns were fought on land, the contest at sea was in the end decisive in accomplishing an English retreat. In 1544 an English military report on the harbours of the Forth, described Inch Garvie as "a pyle or forttres faysible to be wone and a good landinge with schipps or bottes". Accordingly in May of that year Richard Broke, captain of the "Galey Subtile" attacked the island "whiche after a lytell assault made thereunto and some shott out of his galey was rendered unto him." The English King first decided that the fort was worth keeping but then changed his mind and ordered it to be destroyed.

The exact implications for North Queensferry of an enemy power in such close proximity are unknown. Presumably our promontory was fortified and therefore able to repel attacks. The fact that the fortifications on Inch Garvie were reduced seems to suggest that the English were unable or unwilling to hold it and there is no record of the ferry link being interrupted, although the ferry boats can hardly have been a match for the "Galey Subtile" while it was in the vicinity.

In December 1547 however, the ferry service was severed. Sir John Luttrell had been left to guard Inch Colm and used it for a base for harrying the neighbouring coastal towns. He sent a six oared boat to North Queensferry one night and succeeded in capturing the ferry boat "hard by the town". It was estimated that the captured boat would carry 80 men. Two days previously he had burned a house at the town's end in Aberdour, but the people rose so fast that he had to retire. To cap it all on Christmas Day night 1547 he gave them a "camysado" at the North Ferry, and "burned the town and the geldings of the men who fled in haste." From Sir John's point of view it all sounds very sporting and a mention in dispatches must have been gratifying. But from the villagers' point of view, losing their dwellings and horses can only have meant disaster.

North Queensferry was unlucky to have been drawn into the theatre of war, but almost equally unfortunate in simply sitting on the side lines. What the enemy hadn't destroyed, the Government needed for the war effort. In this respect, however, North Queensferry was no worse off than

Inch Garvie September 1981

hundreds of other villages. In June 1548, for instance, after the first sight of the French navy, the villagers were to thresh the corn and bring victuals to the town of Edinburgh. Alexander Forster was to pass to the Queensferry for a cable, probably needed to tow guns. In the same year, an officer was sent to arrest certain timber and tows in the Queensferry, and later a Dutch and a Norwegian vessel were arrested. The same year Peter Smith was sent for two long cables. We can guess that such requests were not always willingly met. But the greatest resistance seems to have been put up to the supply of the most precious commodity of all: men. With the memory of Christmas 1547 fresh in the villagers' minds, this is hardly surprising. In 1548, for instance, a messenger was sent to Queensferry "with ane act furth be the lords charging all men to rys at the sycht of the balis and cum fordvart to Edinburght for the resisting of the Inglische men". Some days later another messenger was sent "witht the fyre croce to the Queenis Ferre, Kinroschire, and Fyſ". Again, all the boat men and the ferrymen of the Forth with their boats were "to cum and fraucht the Francheman and Duche oure the water". The next year the Government sent "in all haiste about to Quennis Ferre because that Inchekeith wes in the Inglischemannis handes to caus all botis langis the coist syde to cum to Abirladye to ressave chargis towart the Inche". There follow two similar orders. An order given on the 2nd of July 1549 explains why so many orders were sent for men and boats. Alexander Forster was sent to Queensferry and several other Forth ports "to summond all marinaris havand bottis quha war absent at the recovering of Inche Keith to underlie the law in Edinburght". The

come to Leith within 3 hours "under the pain of escheating .... and punishing to the deid".

On top of the repeated demand for stores, ships and men, and despite the destruction of the village, the villagers were still expected to operate the ferries, or alternatively suspend operation if this were advantageous for the pursuit of war. At the beginning of the war, the Lord Governor had sent Adam Forman to the Ferrymen of Queensferry and Kinghorn with a letter charging them to help "ower the quenis gracis liegis .... upoun ane resonable fracht". That this letter was necessary in the first place reminds us of the difficulty of communications in the 16th century. It also stresses the importance which the central authority attached to the ferries for the quick movement of troops.

In 1548 a ban on ferrying people over the water was lifted, only to be reimposed a few weeks later "to caus the said ferriaris to stop the ferries for away passing of the Northland men". The same order had been given in 1523. Right down to the rebellions of 1715 and 1745 the Highlanders had an understandable but annoying tendency to wish to return home once their campaigning season was ended. In 1548 an English spy appears to have been taken at Queensferry. A certain Davidson was to produce "ane Inglischman takin by him in wemennis clathis". Another entry threatens Davidson with a £1,000 fine should he fail to

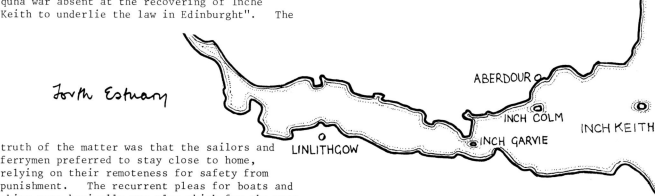

truth of the matter was that the sailors and ferrymen preferred to stay close to home, relying on their remoteness for safety from punishment. The recurrent pleas for boats and ships were basically one plea which for the most part appears to have gone unheeded. But the Government became more and more insistent. In early January yet another order came this time for boats to carry munitions towards the seige of Broughty (Broughty Ferry). This was repeated on the 6th January, and again on the 12th "for marinalis to pass furthe witht John Bartane upon the Inglische schippis that war in Tay lyand to victuall and furnis Broughtye". But our men were limpets and so were the other seamen of the Forth ports. Five days later an order arrived for all the boats and to bring them to the pier of Dundee this night. Whether this appeal for immediate action was successful is unclear. Nevertheless shortly afterwards, Broughty was taken. Now the mariners were needed to expel the English further. There must have been a considerable reluctance to support the Government even at this late stage for in 1550 on the eve of the final expulsion of the English, a final desperate threat was delivered to the mariners of the Forth ports (including Queensferry), for the seamen to

comply. By June 1549 Inchkeith had been recaptured and it was necessary to refortify it "for resisting of our old enemeis". For this work 400 pioneers were necessary, so a list was drawn up of the neighbouring Forth ports. They were to supply labour at 2 shillings a day for 16 days. Both Quenesferie and North Ferrie appear on the list. Finally in the same month a boy was sent with a writing to the Queensferry with the pleasant duty which fittingly concludes this section: "to stay the army cuman fordwart .... because the Inglischmen war returnyt hame".

Mary Queen of Scots

Mary Queen of Scots passed over the Queensferry several times. In fact a large part of her six year reign was spent in Royal progresses. Internal communication by land was inconvenient, slow and even dangerous, not least because of her over-mighty subjects. On a few occasions she is reported to have travelled by coach, at that time a revolutionary, rudimentary and probably excruciatingly uncomfortable mode of travel. On many others she rode on horse back. She was a skilled horsewoman. For instance, in October 1566 she rode from Jedburgh to Hermitage and back, a distance of 50 miles in a single day. It is on horseback that we glimpse her crossing the Queensferry - a tall handsome figure, graceful of movement and richly dressed, surrounded by an entourage of courtiers and accompanied by a crowd of lesser dignitaries and domestics. The ferrymen would have been impassive observers of most of the comings and goings at the ferry. Nevertheless the spectacle of the young Queen and her courtiers, on a plane so far removed from their own, would have been a compulsive talking point in the village inn and homes that night, besides a memory for some to carry through the years.

Mary did not come this way on all her journeys Northwards. Sometimes she used the Leith Kinghorn ferry and on others she went to Stirling via her birthplace, Linlithgow. But as often as not when coming to Fife or returning to Edinburgh she would cross here. The Stuarts had a soft spot for Fife, in particular for Falkland Palace which was a holiday home for them. James V rebuilt it and made new stables. James IV, James V and Mary Stuart all came here for hunting and hawking. Accordingly on 11th February 1563 Mary set out on a trip to Falkland crossing the Forth at Queensferry. At

his dagger through the intruder. Instead Chatelard was captured and taken to St Andrews where he was executed. His last words were from Ronsard's hymn to death: "Je te salue heureuse et profitable mort", a romantic end to what in fact may well have been a squalid story. Chatelard is suspected of being a hireling employed by French interests to blacken Mary's reputation. This explanation makes his severe punishment a little easier to understand.

In February 1565 Darnley, with a claim to the English throne almost as good as Mary's, came North to the Scottish court. He lost no time in following Mary into Fife. She had crossed via the Queensferry in mid January en route for Falkland, and was now returning to Edinburgh by way of St Andrews. They met on 17th February 1565 at the home of the laird of Wemyss. She thought Darnley "the properest and best-proportioned long man" she had ever seen. Her nobles were less romantic. They resented the elevation of one of their number particularly such an arrogant and stupid one. Consequently when once married, the young couple had their share of enemies. It was at this time that an order in the Register of the Privy Council under their joint names, sought to regulate the use of the Forth crossings. It notes that rebels and wicked people were passing daily through Lothian, Fife and Angus and also "diverse suspect and wicked persons threatening to overthrow the King and Queen's authority". Therefore the King and Queen and their secret council "have thought

Falkland Palace. 1981

Burntisland in the castle of Rossend the poet Chatelard burst into her private apartments. Mary cried out for help. Her brother Moray ran in and she hysterically begged him to run

meet and convenient to depute and appoint the keeping of the havens and common passages within the said bounds to such persons, their true and faithful subjects as they have best opinion of ...

for the Limekilns and the North Queensferry with the bounds adjacent thereto, the Commendator of Dunfermline .... For the Blackness and all bounds betwixt the same and South Queensferry James Hamilton of Kinkavill. For the said ferry and all the bounds betwixt the same and Cramond, George Dundas of that Ilk".

The events of the rest of Mary's reign read like some Jacobean melodrama. We must pass over two brutal murders, first of Rizzio and then of her husband Darnley, and her subsequent abduction by Bothwell. Forsaken by Bothwell, defeated at Carberry Hill, imprisoned in Edinburgh, we rejoin her at Loch Leven where she was held captive in late June 1567 until her escape. Early on in her stay she miscarried and during her recovery from this was forced to resign the throne in favour of her son, who was crowned James VI. Mary's health, which had been shattered by the succession of blows, began to improve, in time for her captor's brother, George Douglas, to fall in love with her. From then on an escape became possible, and in May 1568 it became a reality. On 2nd May, Mary, dressed as a country woman, openly crossed the courtyard of the castle. Willy Douglas, a younger member of the Douglas family, had by then obtained the keys to the castle main gate, allowing her to pass through. Outside the castle walls, Mary was recognised by washer women but luckily they kept silent. She then descended to the waiting boat, and here she hid under the boatman's seat during the crossing to the other shore. On the other side she was welcomed by George Douglas and by John Beaton who had stolen the best horses from the stables. Two miles distant she made rendezvous with the Lords Seaton and Riccarton who rode with her to Queensferry. On this her final crossing of the strait Mary would have been exultant both to have escaped and to get another throw of the dice, besides being heartily relieved to put the waters of the Forth between her and her pursuers. Once over the Queensferry, the likelihood of recapture must have seemed remote. For the time being at least, she was safe.

Troubles

There is something stifling about the atmosphere of the Scottish court during the 16th century. This was a time of plots, cloak and dagger politics, cabals and rebellions. Power was the glittering prize and the leaders of society were scrambling in the mire to get it. "Poignarder a l' Ecossais" was a term used in France to denote a killing by repeated dagger strokes. Rizzio received 50 or 60 such wounds, his murderers passing the knife from hand to hand so that all were implicated. The murderers of the Earl of Moray in the reign of James VI did likewise.

At Queensferry, the wind blowing with its accustomed freshness, the air was clearer. At a few miles removed from the court and even further down the social scale, the ordinary folk got on with the everyday business of living. They were keen to exploit their lucrative little monopoly of working the water passage - not that things were always plain sailing, even at Queensferry. In 1571, the Register of the Privy Council records the complaint of John Gardell, Englishman, alleged owner of the ship "Phoenix". He complained that John Moubray had illegally detained his ship which was "lying at the

Queenes Ferrie .... to the gryt skayth and heirschip of the said James" Moubray was charged to bring the "Phoenix" to Leith within 48 hours and when he failed to do this he was charged again to do so under pain of paying the penalties of rebellion. This was not the first time that a Moubray had fallen foul of his sovereign.

Although Queensferry was miles from the court, the river crossing continued to be of immense strategic importance so that the villagers were drawn unwillingly into national events. The most celebrated feuding incident of this period demonstrates both the cynicism of James VI and the brutality of his earls. This was the episode which ended in the death of the Earl of Moray at Donibristle in February 1592. What Moray's offence had been is unclear. Folk tradition suggests an illicit liaison with the Queen:

"He was a braw gallant
And he played at the glove
And the bonnie Earl of Moray
Oh he was the Queen's love".

But it seems that the feud with the Earl of Huntley was a more important factor in bringing about his death. In February 1592 Huntley crossed the Queensferry with 40 followers on horseback. According to reports, the boats had been ordered by the King to be in readiness. Huntley and his followers arrived at Donibristle at midnight and surrounded the house. Moray and the defendants made several sallies killing numbers of attackers who eventually "Took the corn stooks and led to the house so that the extremity of fire drove out the defenders". Moray is reported to have been so burned "that he was not able to hold a weapon in one of his hands". Nevertheless, "he came through them all with his sword in his hand and like a lion forced them all to give place". But valour was no match for numbers. On the beach he was surrounded by his assailants. They struck him down, each taking a turn to strike a blow. As he lay dying he is reported to have accused Huntley of spoiling a bonnier face than his own.

Two letters in the Calendar of Scottish Papers cast a dubious light on the King's part in this episode. Apparently Moray had gone to Donibristle to await Lord Ochiltree who "was to have met him .... and for that purpose came to the ferry and would have gone over but commandment had come thither, as they said from the King, that no boats should pass". On hearing the ferry was stopped, Ochiltree returned to the King "praying the King's warrant for his immediate passage". But the King denied any stoppage at the ferry, and asked Ochiltree to stay that day and the next and "carried him on hunting". The hunting expedition was on the southern shore of the Forth and they both saw a fire at Donibristle. The King asked what place is that? Whereat Ochiltree was amazed and craved leave to go to the rescue. James was adamant however, and ordered him to remain. Following this incident the King admitted giving a "blank commission" to Huntley, which was no doubt a euphemism for a death warrant.

This piece of cynical deceit had been made possible by the King's power first to provide a ferry passage for Huntley, and then to deny it to Ochiltree; so that in the murder of Moray the Queensferry passage played a crucial part. This is not to accuse the ferrymen of being accessories to a brutal murder. Their job was to run a ferry service. They did so for the King's enemies, as well as for his friends. The remarkable thing in this instance is that they actually heeded the King's orders — we have so many instances of their disregarding them. But this appears to have been less a reflection on any new inclination to obedience than on the short period of time that their obedience was necessary in order to have Moray murdered.

The plague

In 1580 a ship arrived in the Forth carrying people "infectit with the pest and sum of thame alredy deid of that same seikness". A proclamation was made in the merchant and fishing ports of the Forth that the plague stricken were to be strictly confined to Inch Colm: forbidding the local people giving help on pain of death. In 1584 a severe outbreak of plague occurred in Fife. In order to protect Edinburgh from the spreading infection, the Ferry was closed. Although officially closed, the Ferry remained unofficially open. It was therefore enacted that there should be no passage over the Forth at any point except between Leith and Kinghorn. Officials were despatched to Queensferry to take the sails from the masts of the boats on both sides of the water. No ship owner or skipper was to transport any manner of persons, even those holding special licenses under the "pane of death". Because testimonials and licenses to pass and repass at all ferries had been over generously granted in the past, all were to be null and void unless presented to one of the baillies of Edinburgh. However, such was the demand for crossings and the need for the ferrymen to earn a living, that even these draconian measures failed. This is clear from a repetition of this act shortly afterwards. It noted the continual transporting of persons at the Queensferry, and other ports, and ordained that "thair salbe na passage ower the Forth be the Ferry boittis at ony pairt except onlie betwixt Leith and Pettycur". Again commissioners were to go to Aberdour, Burntisland and Queensferry to take the sails from the masts of the boats.

In 1590 another plague ship arrived in the Forth, and the baillies and provosts of the Forth ports were warned to keep watch night and day to prevent the crews and passengers landing. Finally by the turn of the century, the plague had spread to the south side of the river but Fife was now clear, so the ferrymen were now ordered under pain of death not to transport any persons from the south to the north, except councillors, and such of their Majesties ordinary domestics as had testimonials of being void and clear of the said plague.

In the 16th century it was the practice to find a convenient but uninhabited island to act as an isolation hospital for plague victims. In the next century ships with infected people aboard were moored in St Margaret's Hope. Provided that they stayed on board there was no danger to the local community. In 1625 a ship out of Leith returned home from Danskeene laden with sundry commodities, including the plague. The ship was carried up to St Margaret's Hope at the Queensferry until the ship had been inspected and shown to be free of the plague. Three years later a ship of Dundee carrying the plague arrived in Leith Roads and then sailed to above the Queensferry where the crew "comes a land at thair pleasure and hantes the companie of cleene people". They were warned on pain of death to keep to the ship. In addition a proclamation was read at the market crosses of all the towns on both sides of the river ordering the inhabitants to keep such people and their goods apart from the local community. A few years later commissioners were appointed by the Government to prevent the landing of plague stricken ships from the Low Countries: "Dundas, his eldest son, and George Dundas of Maner for the Queinsferrie". And in 1645 the historian Chalmers thinks there may have been a plague burial ground at North Queensferry at the North end of Port Laing. He notes a large bluish stone, like a grave stone lying at sea water mark, having on it distinctly the letter S and below this the date 1645", the year in which a great plague hit Dunfermline.

Thankfully the plague is long since gone and so unfortunately is the commemorative stone. We noted earlier the locational advantages of North Queensferry. Now we see some of the counter-vailing disadvantages — first we see the village was used as a link in a cordon sanitaire to prevent the plague reaching Edinburgh from the North, and later it was used to prevent the plague from travelling in the opposite direction. Whichever way the plague was travelling the Ferrymen were exposed to infection if any of their fares were carrying it. As a sea port the village was exposed to additional risks of foreign vessels carrying the plague. Finally the authorities decided that St Margaret's Hope was a good place for stricken vessels to ride at anchor. It was conveniently distant from Edinburgh, Leith and Dunfermline which was what mattered. Its proximity to North Queensferry was regrettable, but this mattered much less. Down the centuries the North end of the peninsula, Inch Garvie and St Margaret's Hope have all been used as quarantines and lazarettos. In a sense, the recent siting of the sewage works for Dunfermline's effluent on ground reclaimed at St Margaret's Bay is therefore part of a long and dishonourable tradition.

Deceits, disputes and the law

It has been estimated that on the eve of the Reformation the Crown's income was only about £17,500 per annum, but the Church's income amounted to at least £300,000. The King had to nurture his meagre revenues and to seek whatever means were at his disposal to supplement them. In November 1571 the Lord Regent sent a messenger to the Ferrie to instuct the owners of the ships to unload wine at Leith only. Presumably it was easier to collect customs duties there. That merchants were evading these duties is clear from an Act of April 1602 concerning the due payment on goods exported and imported. The Act relates to many Forth ports including Queensferry. Apparently merchants were submitting their goods to receive the cocket seal upon them (evidence of having paid His Majesty's custom) and then carrying other goods, no doubt of greater value, without paying dues. This Act forbade the loading or unloading of ships at certain ports (Queensferry included) except for salt, coal, victuals and timber under the pain

Donibristle House, September 1980

of confiscating the whole merchandise.

Coastal places always have a proud history of
smuggling: our own is no exception. In 1610
at South Queensferry the vessel "The Grace" was
unloaded "quietlie, craftilie and undewtifullie",
the persons involved preferring "thair filthy
lucre and gayne to the obedience of the law".
In 1618 we find that masters, owners, and farmers
of saltpans and "coilheughis" upon the water of
the Forth above Queensferry bargain unlawfully
with merchants to relieve them of customs duties
"quilk custome they adjoine to the price of thair
coill and salt". The masters of merchant vessels
practised a different trick: pretending they were
bound for an inland port but "when they are down
the firth and in their opinion out of all suspicion
to be challenged they set their course directly for
England, France, Flanders, or some other port
beyond the sea". Much later in 1686 we find
George Dundas, skipper of the "Dragon" of Queensferry, a prisoner in the Tolbooth in Edinburgh for
not having reported to the customs officer on his
return from Holland to the Ferry. The petitions
for his release were on the grounds that this
omission was committed merely out of ignorance.
These represent the few references to those found
guilty of smuggling, but no doubt many more
evaded the customs without being found out, but
of this multitude no trace remains.

Another way of raising money was by Acts of
Caution. In 1603 permission was given to
Mr John Dawlinge, advocate for John Dawlinge,
master of a ship called the "Mariflour of the
Quenisferre" to sail with her out of the said
harbour where she lies, to sail to the ports of
Denmark and Danskene only, under the pain of 1,000
merks." The king might also take economic
advantage from his subjects' belligerence. In
April 1597 the King took 1,000 merks from
Harry Stewart of Craigiehall and from John Wilson
and William Allan, baillies of South Queensferry ,
not to harm George Dundas of that ilk and members
of his family. With equal-handed impartiality
he took the same amount from David Dundas of
Preistisinche for George Dundas of that ilk and

his sons not to harm the inhabitants of the
Queensferry.

North and South Queensferry being ports and
ferry terminals saw a lot of activity. Such
coastal places have a reputation for commotions
and affrays: the result of altercations between
ferry boatmen and the passing travellers, or
simply the natural consequences of a sailor
drinking too deep in the local inns. We only
begin to hear of these incidents in the 17th
century but presumably they had been part and
parcel of the village life for centuries.
Indeed they are not unknown today.

In 1618 for instance, Robert Hill, mariner in the
ferry attacked Thomas Townis first striking on
his door with "a long great kent" and "wes resolvit
in his beistlie raige to have slaine the said
Thomas". Luckily Thomas was saved by his
wife who was also hurt in the fray. John
Logie, Baillie arrived on the scene but Hill used
disgraceful language (of which unluckily we have
no record) kicked him and pulled out a lot of
his beard. Later Hill succumbed and was
lodged in South Queensferry Tolbooth. He was
fined 300 merks to keep the peace. Two years
later Alexander Ker, Patrick Davie, William Day
and John Cesford appeared before the Regality
Court in Dunfermline charged with assaulting
and wounding Partrick Barber as he and others
were crossing in one of the ferry boats. This
time we know that one Robert Whyte a passenger
used appalling language. To be precise he
shouted "Ruithirowt". But it is unclear why
this should have roused the accused to such a
pitch that they "put violent hands on the said
Robert and reft and rugged his cloak fra him and
have almost casing him in the sea". It must
have been a fearful imprecation. At this
point another ferry boat seems to have come
alongside to mediate between the warring
factions. But "they strook at the boatmen
in Burgane's bot wt wands and hurt and woundit
the sd. Patrick in the face". Before the
court Patrick was able to produce a bloody
napkin as evidence and showed "the mark and

cicatrice thairof on his face". The culprits
who may well have been ferrymen, were found
guilty of "ryot and blode" and were remitted
for sentence to the Lord Chancellor.

On the other side of the river on 15th July
1628 a more spectacular commotion occurred when
Linlithgow sent two baillies to collect customs
at the village's annual fair. The villagers
listened to the customars' speech but then one
of them picked up a piece of stuff from one of
the stalls in lieu of customs. He refused to
give it back but instead "drew ane long dirke".

be put to the horn and escheat". (That is to say
if he failed to pay the fine his goods would be
forfeited and he would be outlawed or expelled
from the town.) From the Tolbooth, Michael
Scot petitioned the King that a summons be taken
out against his assailants. The petition is
addressed "Halyrudhous" and marked "Fiat ut
petitur": (do what is petitioned) but how this
incident was resolved is not recorded.

On the South side in 1637 two ferrymen,
one called George Binks (interestingly in the
time of Queen Margaret this was the name of the

The High Street and Mid Terrace
South Queensferry

This seems to have been almost literally fatal.
About 40 villagers "with bandit stalffes drawin
swords and battouns cruellie sett upon the poore
harmelesse customars, dang the said Charles on his
backe, and by the heid and feete harled him east
the street and doune ane wynd again by hand and
feete like a beast" and eventually threw him in
the Tolbooth. This was a man of 78 and "so
birsed as he may not stirre bot lyes bedfast
spitting blood to the great hazard of his lyffe".
For this the baillies of South Queensferry were
imprisoned in the Tolbooth in Edinburgh.

On 9th July 1631 Michael Scot of Leslie
complained to the Privy Council that John Aitkine
had lain in wait for him at Dunfermline.
Catching up with him on the way to Queensferry
he assaulted him from behind with "a great
sting", gave him a number of wounds on the head
and felled him to the ground. John Aitkine
explained that beforehand Scot had attacked
him with a staff "to the great effusion of blood".
Scot was ordered to the Tolbooth, Edinburgh and
"there remain until order be taken with him for
this insolence and failing to do so he is to

rock where passengers landed at South Queensferry),
were brought before the baillies and convicted
of injuring each other. The sentence was
worthy of Solomon. Each was fined £5, to be
paid by one to the other and "ye said persons to
end in friendship and to drink togedder and ye
said George Binks to drink first to ye
said John Blair in respect he did ye greatest
violence".

Five years later a disagreement over the
sale of a horse terminated far less amicably.
Arnot, Laird of Fairnie came to Queensferry to
buy a horse but was not pleased with the price
at which one was offered by Andrew Gray. The
Laird gave vent to his frustration by calling
Gray's son-in-law "knave and lowne". The latter
"modestly excepted against those speeches", drew
his sword and "therewith almost mutilat him in
the hand" and thereafter gave him a "deep stog
stroke" on the thigh . Gray tried to separate
them but his son-in-law was wounded in the
shoulder and struck the ground.

One of the most picturesque local squabbles

occurred in January 1684 at South Queensferry between James Hill, Baillie of South Queensferry and George Dawling, skipper there "after they hade come from their recreatione on the ice". Hill was allegedly a difficult character. Dawling accused him of having "drunk too liberally". He "upbraided the haill incorporatione of skippers and seamen by calling them sones of whoors and beggarly doges for buying a passadge boat called David with the seamen's box". Dawling remonstrated, so Hill took the tongs out of the chimney to beat him and threw Dawling's cape "a sabble fur" into the fire. For these assaults Dawling paid Hill a return visit and gave him "many bauch, blae and bloody stroakes to the perril and danger of his lyfe". Dawling was found guilty and ordered to pay 200 merks to the King and 100 merks to Hill. Finally in 1686 a confusing episode occurred involving a pair of pistols in which George Steill one of his Majesty's waiters was attacked by desperate rogues. The baillies of South Queensferry were summoned to Edinburgh to explain this lapse in local discipline and "to bring alongst with you Charlie, a woman who lives in the Ferrie".

In these troubled times the perils at home may have been dire but they were small relative to the dangers of venturing to sea. In 1608 Robert Hill, Skipper in the Queensferry, petitioned the King concerning a Dutch war ship which had captured his merchant vessel carrying coal between Culross and Gravelines and had thrown the crew overboard to perish. The King wrote to the Estates of the United Provinces for redress. The next year Ninian McMorane and James Arnot petitioned the King to obtain compensation amounting to £1,500 English for the loss of their ship, "The James" of Queensferry. They accused William King, proprietor of "The Elizabeth" of Newcastle, of "overthrawing and drowneing of thair schip and of the haill merchandice". In 1628 Edward Paterson and John Bynkes, sometime dwellers in the Queensferry and now prisoners in Dunkirk appealed to the Privy Council for help. An incident in 1625 shows that mariners could not even rely on people on land for help in an emergency. A Queensferry vessel, "The Gift of God" was returning home from France laden with wine but was driven by contrary wind and storm into the Mouth of the Tweed where the ship was "cassin away". The wines were lost and all but two of the crew drowned. At one point a hawser was thrown from the ship "to half fasnit hir witheupoun land" but the locals cut it, such was their "inordinate desire for spoils and gain". The ship was exposed to the merciless rage of the sea and the wreckers took what they could of the ship's gear, cargoes and ordinance. Finally in 1633 "The George" of Queensferry was seized by a Spanish freebooter All the crew were taken prisoner and put under decks. One half of them was released in mid channel: the other half was imprisoned and ill treated in San Sebastian and petitioned the King for their release.

Closer to home it was necessary to keep the channels clear above Queensferry to allow passage for merchant vessels. In 1623 the masters and skippers of vessels using the Firth petitioned the King to appoint "ane speciall honest man" to superintend ships using the narrow waters above Queensferry and to prevent them from discharging ballast there. Coal and salt exporters took on ballast for the journey back to Scotland. They discharged it in the Forth and this caused sand banks and obstructions by which the ships were "gritumlie damnifiet". Accordingly in 1630 the King appointed commissioners to see fair play and the next year they reported that the discharge of ballast was still a serious problem causing obstruction and making it difficult to find anchorage. In the same year we have a list of names of skippers in the Forth towns who found the King's action in planning a light house on the May Island "most royall and just and prosecution thereof most expedient and necessar for the weale of his subjects". David Wilson and William Lowry signed for the Queensferry.

Managing the Queensferry Passage: an early attempt

In 1589 James VI married Queen Anne of Denmark. North Queensferry was amongst the East coast towns to provide masters and mariners to bring the Queen from Norway. The Queen had an even closer association with this village because she received the Queensferry Passage as a wedding gift from her new husband. How the Passage had found its way in the King's hands is a mystery. At the time of the Reformation it had been administered by a lay commendator in succession to the Abbot of Dunfermline. Chambers explains that in the year after James VI's wedding "it was disposed of to a joint stock company, the first thing of the kind perhaps known in Scotland and of which a very amusing anecdote is told. The Abbot being very anxious to raise money and afraid moreover that all his property would soon be wrested out of his hands, gave a hasty order to an agent to dispose of the Ferry if not to one person to as many persons as could agree in clubbing together for the purchase. The agent accordingly divided the Ferry into 16 shares and offered them for sale. The project was immediately successful. The shares were eagerly purchased; the agent continued to sell as long as he had found persons willing to buy and succeeded in selling 18 sixteenth shares of the Queensferry Passage".

We know that the sixteen proprietorial shares related to land on either side of the Ferry, as well as to the Ferry itself: four shares related to land on the Ferryhills, the other twelve to more extensive land on the South side known as Muiryhall. The proprietors leased out the Passage to crews who paid them an annual rent out of what they could make from the "fraughts". These had been fixed in 1559 as follows:

ilk man and horse	8 pence
ilk man or woman be themself	4 pence
any boit be himself to pay for his porterage	4 shillings

In 1598 a common box of North Queensferry was appointed for "collecting of ane penny of everie manner of fraught in ye day" to help the needy. The villagers saw fair play by setting down that the box was to be opened periodically "in the presence of ye haill honest men of ye toun". There seems to have been some doubt about the supply of such paragons of virtue for the quotation goes on .... "or at least in the presence of sex or sevin of ye maist honest men of ye said toun". The contents were to be distributed to the needy.

The same year, Harry Thomson and John Burgane, owners of the new boat at North Ferry laid a complaint before the Regality Court, Dunfermline concerning abuses committed by John Cant and Andrew Thomson on the ferry passage. The court discerned:

"that in all tymes coming yr sall nane of ye handlars and travellaris in ye said boitt transporte ye samyn fray ane syde of ye ferry to ye uyir with na fewar number in fiar weddar nor sex habill hands and in ye tyme of wintar and rouche weddar with na fewar nor sevein habill persounis excep'd ye said Harry Thomsoun or ye said John Burgane elder be yair in ye boitt or any of yame".

Another form of abuse reached the ears of the Privy Council in 1621. On 6th November John Smeaton was crossing the passage on business having "agreeit with the skipper and company of the boitt callit Fortoun for his fraught". After they had almost crossed he offered his fare but it was refused. "And then Thomas Millair ane of the company of the said boitt gaif him a number of cruell straikis behind his bak, or evir he wes awar of him, with the taill of ane grite tow, upon the head, faice, shoulders and utheris partis of his body and gaif him tua cruell woundis with the said tow upon the head". They also took his sword and his "quhinger" which they retained at the time of Smeaton's appeal to the Privy Council. The result of the appeal was that Thomas Millair was found guilty in his absence and sentenced to 6 days in the Tolbooth of Edinburgh on pain of horning.

Many were the trials of the passenger making the short crossing at Queensferry. In 1622 there is reference to "insolence committed by one of the Waughteris (Dunkirk) ships against a Ferry boat crossing the Ferry". In 1633 Charles I crossed further down stream "in grat jeopardy of his lyffe". One of the boats sank carrying several of his servants and his household silver. Then

on Lammas Day 1634 "bright weather and no wind, the best boat of the Queensferry was through want of skill wrecked on Inchgarvie with loss of goods, the passengers being saved at great hazard". In the same year another was swept downstream and wrecked on Cramond Island with loss of all lives.

The impression given is that our ferrymen were not only rogues, but incompetent rogues. With the advantage of close personal experience this is what the King thought. In July 1635 he wrote a letter from his court at Bagshot to the Privy Council complaining that "persons and goods are sometimes cast away .... by the unskilfulness and the disorderly way of ferrymen who have no order at all .... rather practise what may tend to their own lucre .... their trade being promiscuouslie carried out and without respect to breeding or skill".

Twelve years later with the threat of invasion the Privy Council made preparations by improving the country's fortifications and communications. The ferry landing places (probably still the Binks on the South Side) were inconvenient and dangerous. The Privy Council decerned that the skippers of ferry boats should uplift the following charges to be put in a box for financing the repair of these landing places,

ilk duke, earl viscount	3 shillings 4 pence
ilk lord	1 shilling 8 pence
for ye man or woman	1 penny
ilk horse cow or ox	2 pence
ilk twenty sheep	4 pence

this money was known as "The Ferry Silver". We meet it again later.

Those who owned the feus of the Ferry Passage on either side of the water had certain obligations:

to keep good and sufficient boats to work the passage

to man them with adequate and skilled crews

to provide proper "bridges" or "ganges" for those embarking or disembarking

to provide accommodation for horses, cows and other beasts

We know that they failed on several of these counts, in their greater concern for the benefits than for the obligations of ownership. In particular too many boats were allowed to compete for custom on the passage. In 1669 things came to a head and by an Act of Parliament of that year the Ferry was brought partly under the control of local sheriffs and Justices of the Peace.

Black Castle, South Queensferry

18

The changes of 1669 started with a familiar complaint to the Regality Court concerning "dissorders and abuses comittat at the sd. Ferrie by the masters and boatmen belonging yrto both ther refusing and giving readie service to the leidges as they have been required. And by ther undiscreet exacting of Fraughts and oyr miscariadges of that nature." The court decided to summon the feu-holders to produce before the court "their rights to the feu of the water of the South and North Ferrie that everyone's several proportions therein may be known". The following appeared:

	Number of sixteenth parts
Archibald Wilson	8
George Hill	4
John Alan)	
Edward Paterson)	
John Moncrieff)	4
Matthew Dawling)	
Robert Hill)	

It was decreed for the better running of the Ferry "that no persone having interest to the sd. watter passage shall put upon the sd. water passage any boat or boats unless they appeir they have interest to the Four sexteine parts of the said water passage and eftir provinn yrof they are to have a speciall autoritie and appoyntment bairin the said boat is allowed by the privillidge of the court to pass in all tymes as one Ferrie boat" the authorised owners and boats were as follows:

Owner	Boat
Archibald Wilson of South Queensferry	"Yesterfriggitt" built in South Queensferry in the previous year
Jeanne Moubray widow of North Queensferry	"Burgane"
John Allane of South Queensferry	"Issobell" and a new boat "Burgane Yoll"

The last-named boat was a yawl and it is interesting to note that one of the cottages in the village is still known as "Yoll Cottage".

Besides regulating the number of boats the court set down a series of rules for the working of the Passage. To start with they amended the charges: a single person was to pay 1/4d. and a single person and a horse 3/4d. Hopefully they added "and this but prejudice to the discretion of any person that shall be pleased to give more". The other rules were as follows:

1. "That no persone presum to transport ane passanger upone the sd. ferrie unless it be in one of the ordinairie passage boats" - belonging to one of the stewards and licensed by the Regality Court.

2. "That no boatman serving at the said passage presume to lay hold upone any gentleman or uyr passanger ther horss to carie ym away to the boat wtout they be particularlie ordained and required yrto by the passangers themselves".

3. "That all boatmen heireftir serve any of the leidges upone all occasiones wind, tyde and weather serving"; a special charge for "ilk passanger that shall happine to be haistand upon any extraordinarie occasion".

4. "That the ordinarie fraught upone any ordinarie passage shall pay as follows viz. a single persone one shilling foure pennies, a single passanger and one horse three shillings four pennies. And this but prejudice to the discretion of any person that shall be pleased to give moir".

5. "That no man or boat presum to transport passages upon the Lords Day either in the tyme of dwyne service or any uyr tyme unless the pairtie be upone some publick concernment and have autoritie ... or if any uyr passager upone the accompt of sickness goieing for any phisician to ane passien provyding they have ane testificatin from the justice of peace magistrate or minister".

6. "That there being onlie two great boats now upone the passage that they shall so contryve ther passage that they may be allwayes one at each syde of the water"

These sensible rules were meant to bring about order. In particular it was hoped that "two great boats .... shall so contrive the passage that they be always one at each side of the water". But the Regality Court could not eradicate in a few months a tradition built up over centuries. The ferrymen continued their abuses; the ferry-owners their exactions. Most of all the law couldn't change the naturally bad conditions of the passage - the winds, the tides and the landing places.

By an Act of Parliament the same year, however, the passage came under the partial control of local officials. The landing places were found to be dangerous, ruinous, "uncommodious" and unsuitable for several times of the tide. Accordingly Sir Alexander Bruce of Broomhall for the North Side and James Dundas of Dundas for the South Side were appointed to supervise work on the shippings and landing places. The actual work was entrusted to Archibald Wilson, Baillie of South Queensferry. By the time he had spent £887-8-6d. on this work the two supervisors had discovered a handy way of paying him. They saw that there was an old custom called the ferry silver "bein in use to be uplifted off the boatmen for beiting and keiping up these landing places .... which custom has been in use to be collected in a box, and expenses of beiting the landing places taken off the first and readiest thereof and superplus payed in to the Fewars and tacksmen of the water passage". As Archibald Wilson still had additional expenses to make before completion of the works, they proposed that the ferry silver be paid immediately to the said baillie. The suggestion was approved by the Lords in Council and the boatmen were ordained to make the payment to Archibald Wilson which can hardly have met with an enthusiastic response amongst them, or the tacksmen. Despite improvements complaints continued. In 1678 the Regality Court decreed that "sailors and boatmen carry themselves decentlie and not upbraid and threaten the patrons they serve". The Lords reiterated that "no boatmen rais ony Fraucht on the people butt the auld fraucht under pain of vi sh". In 1683 the Privy Council admitted that notwithstanding the Act of 1669 for repair of bridges, highways and ferries the said Act "hath taken little or no effect". They ordered an inspection to see that those appointed under the Act were either doing their job or punished for having neglected to do so. No doubt, Sir Alexander Bruce and James Dundas escaped censure. All the same the Privy Council noted that some of the ferries "to the reproach of this age, are become ruinous and others fallen into decay". They went on to invoke the Act concerning Ferries of 1425, a mark perhaps of their despair.

The next year comes a reminder that ferrying across the Forth was becoming a competitive business. While commercial development along the banks of the river meant more business for the existing ferrymen, it might also bring into existence new ferries in new locations. In 1684 the magistrates of Kinghorn and Burntisland, the location of the other principal Forth Ferry, reminded the Privy Council that their people had "past all memory of man, layd out their stockes and bred their people to manadge these great boates .... not one of these great boates having drouned these hundred years" despite the ferry being of an extraordinary breadth. They pointed out how conveniently they had made the arrangements for transhipment and complained bitterly of the running of small competitive ferries in fair weather from Kirkcaldy. Nothing daunted, the magistrates of Kirkcaldy, argued that "it is not intelligible how His Majesty's subjects should

be constricted contrary to their interest and convenience to go and seek passage only at Burntisland". It was not right to discourage an up and coming town like Kirkcaldy which "at this very tyme is building a convenient and commodious harbour".

Life can hardly have been easy for North Queensferry inhabitants in the 17th century. Famine, plague and civil war were extraordinary burdens to be carried on top of the more normal ones of poor food, inadequate shelter and short life expectancy. There was one great and compensating advantage however: the ferrymen, on whom the village relied for much of its income, were their own masters, answerable in theory to a distant authority but in practice to no one. The Privy Council might shut the ferry for a few hours or even days, but they couldn't keep it shut for an extended period. There were always travellers who wanted to cross and ferrymen who were prepared to carry them. In this bargain the devil took the hindmost, for once on board, the traveller was pretty much at the mercy of the ferrymen. If the latter upped the price, it was an unwise traveller who flatly refused to pay. They might find themselves put ashore on Inch Garvie or their belongings left to float in the bay. At the very least they would get an earful of ugly abuse or be intimidated with some fearful threat. These ferrymen may not have known it but this was their hey-day. They didn't give a hang about authority and authority wasn't strong or efficient enough to control them. In 1689 there were eight boats working the passage in outright defiance of the Regality Court's ruling twenty years earlier. Only as the next century progressed was this splendid independence at last to be checked, and even then not finally or conclusively. For the moment the ferrymen looked out on the world as from a peak, not aware of the valleys beyond.

Yoll Cottage and Post Office Lane
Spring 1981

CHAPTER III

War and Witchcraft

Just over a hundred years separate Sir John
Luttrell's destruction of the village, and the
invasion by Cromwell's soldiers. Once again
the village was in the grip of political forces
on a national scale. Queensferry represented a
strategic crossing point. The fortifications of
Inch Garvie which had been pulled down in 1550
were now of crucial importance. There had been
several attempts to re-erect them. In 1632
Charles I had agreed that Alexander, Earl of
Linlithgow and Lord Admiral of Scotland should
build and keep a fort at Inch Garvie on a 19 year
grant in exchange for which he would collect
2/- Scots for every ton of coal or salt exported
via Inch Garvie. Little tangible seems to have
resulted for in 1649 Sir James Hacket was put in
charge of repairing the fortifications. The
next year an importunate Parliament instructed
"that ten bolls of the hundred bolls of Meill
to be furnished by Sir Will Dick to the Castle of
Edr. be carried thither .... and that the
Queensferrie furnish beds, pots and pans. And
the proveist of Edr. to cause furnished furth
of the duke hammiltounes coal patt, ten chalder
of coalls". In June 1650 £555 - a massive sum,
was allocated to Inch Garvie and in December of
the same year Sir James Hackett was officially
designated keeper of Inch Garvie by Act of
Parliament. On New Years Day 1651 Charles I
took personal command of the army. In February
he visited the batteries at Inch Garvie and
North Queensferry. At Inch Garvie he expressed
confidence "that there were none there that would
distrust him, since he had as much at stake as
any of them all forby the oath of God which was
on him as their King, yea their covenanted King".
We have no record of how this little speech was
received. Ominously, however, in March 1651 a
surgeon and a chaplain were appointed to the
island. But by this time 16 large cannon were
in position and supplied with munitions; besides,
the place was well-nigh impregnable.

1650 saw Cromwell in Edinburgh. The remains of
the retreating Scottish army assembled at Torwood,
South of Stirling where reinforcements and
recruits swelled the ranks. The increased
numbers and excellent defensive position "within

bogs and advantages and places inaccessible" made
the Scottish army once more a force to be
reckoned with. Cromwell was now in a quandary.
Should he advance on the well-positioned Scottish
army and risk defeat, or try some flanking move?
If the latter, how could it be accomplished when
the West was impassable and on the East, the
Forth separated him from his opponents? The
English warships under Admiral Deane controlled
the Forth but were unable to enter the well-
protected harbours of Fife. Two attempts on
Burntisland had failed. Anyway, it was too far
to the West to establish a beach head.

Cromwell's advanced base was at Linlithgow. From
here he later admitted "we were gone as far as we
could in our council and action; and we did say
to one another we knew not what to do". Soon a
plan began to develop. Admiral Deane had a
flotilla of 55 vessels and flat-bottomed boats.
If he could dominate the Queensferry strait a
force might be landed on the North side.
Accordingly in March 1651 he captured the
Guardship securing the inner harbour of St
Margaret's Hope. Throughout the first six
months of 1651 attacks on Inch Garvie were
frequently repeated but unsuccessful. In view
of the strength of the English flotilla these
must have been severe, fully justifying the money
and care spent in rebuilding the fortifications.
By July, however, the English appear to have
crippled the island. But they didn't manage
to take it, as a contemporary report implies:
"the great ships go next the island and shoot
all the while; the boats pass under the wing and
receive no harm". Perhaps, the garrison had
run out of munitions. Anyway, between July
13th and 16th the English naval guns were turned
on North Queensferry which had a "great sconce"
or battery, guarding the strait. The scene was
now set for an advance party under Colonel Overton
to cross. The crossing was described in an
English report in the following terms: "we sent
a party in boates and ships over the fryth, from
Blacknesse to surprise North-Ferry on Fife-side;
at the first we sent one thousand four hundred foot,
and two hundred horse, and one troop of dragoons,
it pleased the Lord to go along with them so as

within two houres after their landing they took the place called North-Ferry, which is a peninsula, in which was a fort with five great guns, and in a bay near it four ships laden with coales and salt; in some other forts near it we took as many Ordnance as made up those five to be seventeen, which were planted by the fryth side to gall our ships, this North-Ferry is even against the strong island of Ennisgarvie, we have sent over the sixteen and seventeen days of July five hundred foot more, and five troops of dragoons, if by the Lord's mercy we can make this place good, Ennisgarvy must yield for want of fresh water, and then we have a brave way of possessing our whole army into Fife if we see occasion".

We are not quite sure where this force landed. Bensen argues that the landing probably took place at night, that crossing between Inch Garvie and the North Queensferry batteries would have been foolhardy and that the direct route from Blackness would point to a landing at St Margaret's Bay. Balfour's Annals state that the landing was "at the neucke below the Queins Ferray" which would almost certainly mean at Port Laing, because Inverkeithing inner bay and St James Bay and North Queensferry would have been too well protected. Douglas in "Cromwell's Scottish Campaigns" maintains that the stakes used to tie up the landing craft at Port Laing were still in use in 1882. Such evidence is inconclusive. Stake nets were erected at Port Laing to catch salmon in the 19th century. Douglas may well have mistaken these disused stakes as those of Cromwell's soldiers. Bensen's theory is attractive but St Margaret's Bay was normally well-protected, as befitted one of the largest inner havens on the East Coast of Scotland.

We do know that having landed, the expeditionary force attacked North Queensferry from behind. The batteries of the village pointed to sea and the cannon were fixed. Thus the attack on the village and the capture of 17 cannon were easily accomplished with a loss of only six men. On the night of July 18th and the morning of the next day, Major General Lambert arrived at South Queensferry with two regiments of horse and two of infantry. The crossing which took 36 hours for the four regiments would probably have been made direct to North Queensferry, perhaps, with the unwilling help of the local ferrymen.

In the meantime, on the other side of the country, Cromwell faced the Scottish army. Indeed he attacked the Torwood position on the 17th, hoping to create a diversion while Overton gained a foot hold in Fife. Here is part of his letter dated 21st July from "Lithgow" to the Speaker of the House of Commons: "After our waiting upon the Lord and not knowing what counsel to take (for indeed we know nothing but what God pleaseth to teach us) of his Great Mercy we were directed to send a party to get us a landing by our boats whilst we marched towards Glasgow. On Tuesday morning last Colonel Overton with about 1,400 foot and some horse and dragoons landed at the North Ferry in Fife, we with the army lying near to the enemy (a small river parted us and them) and we having consultation to attempt the enemy within his fortifications but

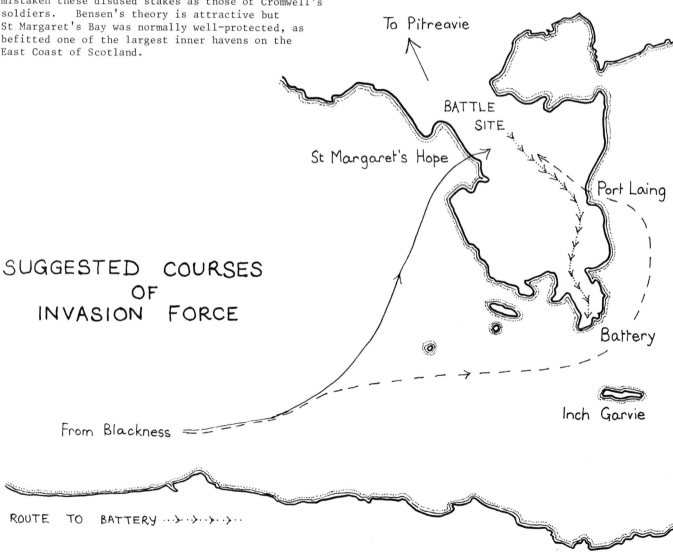

SUGGESTED COURSES
OF
INVASION FORCE

To Pitreavie

BATTLE SITE

St Margaret's Hope

Port Laing

Battery

Inch Garvie

From Blackness

ROUTE TO BATTERY ··>··>··>··>··

the Lord was not pleased to give way to that counsel, purposing a better way for us ....". Thus both the story that he walked to and fro in Barnbougle grounds (South Queensferry) muttering "O God spare Christian blood" and the name of the knoll in North Queensferry on which Craig Dhu stands ("Cromwell's Mount") lack solid evidence. His own letter implies he was elsewhere at the time. He may nevertheless have come to North Queensferry after the battle. (For the solace of those who would not like historical evidence to spoil village traditions.)

An unspeakable mercy

Lambert's position was tenuous but geography was on his side; thirty miles separated him from Torwood and a narrow neck of land separates North Queensferry from the rest of Fife. By the time he arrived the captured cannon from North Queensferry had been dragged across the Ferryhills and repositioned on the Gallow bank facing North. Overton's men "working for their lives to intrench themselves" threw up earthworks across the neck of land. Luckily for the English, an army was not despatched from Torwood until the 19th. It arrived in Dunfermline that evening and the next day advanced to a position on the Salvedge and Castland hills west of Inverkeithing. Even then, Lambert was still bringing the last of his reinforcements over, explaining later that "we stood on our defence till most of ours were come".

The two armies which now faced each other across the valley containing the Great North Road were more or less evenly balanced in numbers. The English army was a contingent of the highly disciplined New Model Army under the single leadership of Lambert. It numbered 4,500 of whom about a quarter were cavalry, the latter of immense importance in 17th century engagements. The Scottish army was smaller, at 4,000 men. It was led by Major General James Holburn and comprised 1,000 cavalry under Sir John Brown, 1,500 Highlanders forming a virtually independent command under Sir Hector Maclean, 100 archers from Perth, 400 "brave but untrained men" from Inverkeithing and 1,000 men from Dunfermline. The difficulty of welding these separate forces into a single army was aggravated by personal tensions amongst the Scottish generals.

Each army had a good defensive position: the other could only be taken by an uphill charge. But the English commander was apprehensive that any moment an even larger force might arrive from Torwood. Having spent the morning of the 20th facing but not fighting the enemy he resolved to take the initiative by assaulting the Scottish position. The disposition of the armies is difficult to deduce from contemporary reports. In each case the strength seems to have been on the right: thus the opening phase of the battle was like a gigantic pivot with the English right wing striking towards Inverkeithing, and the Scots right advancing over the ground now occupied by the motorway roundabout. The English cavalry was on the left of the main English force and divided into two wings. The left was "upon a very ill ground where was a pass lined by the enemy's musketeers"; the right, where the strength lay, consisted of two of Major Lidcot's troops, two of Major Okey's troops and, the regiment of the Major General, all under the charge of Major Okey. It was here that the weight of the Scottish attack fell. The Scots cavalry led

Cromwellian Pike Heads

by Sir John Brown charged the English horse, penetrating the first body and leaving them in such disorder, that English reserves waiting in Welldean quarry, and Lambert's own forces had to intervene to stem the attack. Lambert himself had a horse killed and was hit by musket fire, though not wounded. The weight of the attack however, fell on the right wing of the English cavalry. "The service was very hot at the sword's point and especially with Col Okey's men who had the left to the left and were very hard put to it". The Scottish advantage was short-lived. An English commentator says "their left wing of horse was weak, our strong right wing routed that and after a showre of small shot upon the foot, they all fled and fell like sheep before our men". Certainly the failure of the Scottish cavalry to follow up the early advantage seems to have been crucial. The English cavalry was left to make inroads into the Scottish infantry.

The engagement continued in its heat about a quarter of an hour when according to an English report "the horse being beaten, their foot presently threw away their arms". At this point the battle turned into a rout. Of the Scots army 2,000 were killed and 1,400 captured. The Highlanders made a last desperate stand under the walls of Pitreavie Castle some four miles from the battlefield. Of 800 Maclean fighting in the battle only 40 are said to have survived. Lambert, explaining the large number of Scots killed, wrote "the reason why the number of slain exceeded the number of prisoners was because divers of them were highlanders and received very ill quarter" ie the highlanders fought to the death.

Cromwell described the English victory as "an unspeakable mercy; I trust the Lord will follow it until he hath perfected peace and truth". He had every right to be pleased; he had captured the mortally wounded Sir John Brown, taken 40 or 50 colours destroyed a vital part of the Scottish army and outflanked the Scottish position at Torwood - all for the loss of 8 men and many wounded (at least these were the figures quoted by the English, no doubt for propaganda purposes). Unspeakable it may have been, but little mercy was shown - at least not to the Scots. The Pinkerton burn which crosses the valley in which the conflict took place is supposed to have run red with blood for three days and the battlefield was like a "hairst field with corpses", ie thickly strewn with new cut sheaves. These local reactions were well justified. The English pursuit deteriorated into a brutal slaughter. An English report records that "of their foot not 200 escaped and those that are prisoners the most of them are so desperately wounded they will hardly live". Slaughter on the field was followed by plunder of the towns and countryside, notably in Inverkeithing itself, Spencerfield and Rosyth Castle. The Dunfermline Kirk session records read "the boord and seats of the session-hous and the kirk boxe being all broken and the haill money in the said boxe being all plunderit and taken away by Cromwell's men".

Reformation and Presbyterianism penetrated even to the ferrymen. The penalty noted above for a second offence was similar to that meted out to the unchaste, who had to appear in the "seck gowne" at the "repentance seat". So intense was the use of these that both had to be repaired on several occasions in the 17th century. Terrible were the professions of innocence: "I do solemnly call God to be a witness against me and to take vengeance on me if I have sworn falsely by making me a fugitive and a vagabond in the earth .... that the great and terrible God may treat me as His enemy and as a blasphemer and profaner of His name and

Spencerfield, by Inverkeithing

Six days after the battle, the garrison at Inch Garvie finally gave in. Cromwell's letter implies that the defenders escaped or were allowed to go free; "they marched away with their swords and baggage only leaving us sixteen cannon and all their other arms and ammunition". Following the battle Cromwell advanced again on the Torwood position with no success. He therefore shipped his main force over at Queensferry in order to strike at the enemy from the East. Within weeks, however, the Scottish army had embarked on its fatal invasion of England. Cromwell followed them South, leaving a series of small garrisons to hold Scotland, and no regrets at his departure.

Religious beliefs and persecutions

The Inverkeithing Kirk session records of the 17th century reveal the church as an ubiquitous moral guardian at a time of stern and uncompromising religious beliefs. Extracts from the session records convey the religious and moral atmosphere of the time. In 1635 for instance, the kirk ruled that "whatsoever persons shall break the Sabbath Day by sailing their great or small boats to ply this ferry from the rising of the sun to the twelfth hour of the day, these persons shall be fined for the first fault in twelve shillings Scots the man, and they shall fail in the same fault any time they shall stand at our kirk door in sack cloth and make confession of their fault before the congregation. If the masters of the boats be agents to the boatmen, they shall pay five pounds". Thus the influence of the Scottish

may overthrow and overwhelm me in His wrath and fierce anger". Even more terrible was excommunication: "we cast him out of the Church of God .... we deliver him to Satan to the destruction of the flesh, we bind his sin upon him ...."

For contemporary believers these words had an awful reality. When we also take into account the prevalence of plague, and its capricious incidence on top of all the other uncertainties of 17th century life, the hysteria of witch hunts becomes a little more understandable. Witch hunts occurred in both Inverkeithing and South Queensferry, so presumably victims were also found here. The position of a suspect was perilous as is shown by the supplication to the Privy Council of Mary Young, daughter of John Young, mariner in South Queensferry. Writing on the 8th August 1644 she says "I have been kept since the first of April last and watched as some notorious malefactor in the tolbooth of the Queensferry by the procurement of the baillies and minister there, upon misinformation by my unfriends that I am guilty of witchcraft, howbeit most innocent of the same ....". She asks for her imprisoners to bring her to trial or to set her free. As a result the baillies and minister were summoned to the Privy Council in Edinburgh. In "evidence" there it transpired that her mother, aunt and sister had all been burnt for witchcraft and that she too was judged a witch according to the confession of five other witches, all of whom had been burnt, after having given their incriminating evidence.

Confessions and accusations were easily obtained by using the "brodders" - a set of needles used for probing for the "devils mark", a spot on the body which was insensitive to pain. John Kincaid of South Queensferry took "upon him at his own hand without warrant or order to prick and try these persons who are suspect to be guilty of the abominable crime of witchcraft". Torture, imprisonment, and long interrogations without sleep inevitably produced both confessions and accusations. The penalty was for the victim to be strangled and her remains burnt. On our side of the water this took place at Witch Knowe, a plot close to where the Episcopalian Church of St. Peter now stands. It is to the South of the church on the same side of the main road to Inverkeithing.

In April 1649 the Synod of Dunfermline was informed that some went superstitiously to wells "denominat for Saintis". The purpose was to appeal to the spirit of the place and to use the water for curing illness, almost certainly the plague. The Kirk was opposed to such superstitions. Despite this, people in a place like the Ferry may well have attached healing properties to the local wells. The old well known as Willies Well on the South side of the main road just above the shore, has a tradition attaching to it that those who drink from it will return to the Ferry. It may well have had some more important symbolic significance in days gone by.

Willies Well

Without a local church (the village church had been abandoned and the nearest was St Peter's, Inverkeithing) the people of the Ferry were remote from the religious authorities. In 1695 the people in the North Ferry were "admonished publickly by the minr. not to passe in boats upon the Sabbath Day and also not to carrie in their water as formerlie". We can deduce from this that the Kirk rule of 1635 had been flagrantly

broken. We can judge too by similar Kirk session entries in 1697 and 1736 that the rule was persistently broken. The church authorities nevertheless strove to enforce higher standards. For instance, in 1721, Margaret Stenhouse was rebuked by the Kirk Session and recommended to behave better in the future. She admitted that she had "followed after the soldiers to the North Ferrie". Her offence was "a light and unsuitable carriage".

The restoration of Charles II in 1662 ended the Cromwellian dictatorship. The new King declared a "liberty to tender consciences" which was to heal religious differences. The reality was somewhat different. He appointed bishops and relegated the spiritual power of the church to the secular power of the State. Only church ministers who acceded to the superior power of a bishop could retain their livings. As a result 270 ministers were expelled from their parishes. Many continued to carry out their duties in secret, and at field conventicles (open-air services).

The heritors of North Queensferry would not sign the bond of peace forbidding conventicles. Indeed a field conventicle was held close to the village in 1678. South Queensferry was a well-known centre of recusancy. For this reason troops were quartered there - both to keep the peace and to penalise the residents. At this time the Ferry was watched for the comings and goings of "suspect persons with arms". Following the defeat of the rebels at Bothwell Bridge (1679) the ferry was temporarily closed. Several rebels were subsequently captured and held at South Queensferry. The next year some of these escaped and local people were suspected of aiding them. As a result several South Queensferry residents sustained large monetary penalties. The Privy Council also ruled "Katherine Robertson to be scourged through the town of Queensferry on Friday next by the hangman".

As far as we can tell penalties on the people of North Queensferry were less severe but still very considerable. In 1676 James Henderson, innkeeper of North Queensferry, was declared a rebel and had his goods forfeited for attending conventicles. Robert Dick in North Ferry and Robert Townes, a seaman there, were fined 300 pounds each for similar offences. In September 1678, John Harrower was arraigned before the Privy Council for having preached at conventicles and having exercised the functions of the ministry at several places including North Queensferry. In 1680, Donald Cargill, a leading Presbyterian was arrested at South Queensferry, carrying the Queensferry paper. This was a tract denouncing bishops, the relegation of spiritual power to that of the state, idolatry, popery and attacking the "indulged" ministers. Cargill escaped. Brock notes that James Henderson, a boatman of North Queensferry, was an accomplice in trying to capture Cargill and that following Cargill's escape his boat, "bought with blood money", was boycotted. We know that Henderson was a Presbyterian. It seems unlikely therefore, that he would have been helping to capture Cargill. Perhaps he was pretending to do so as a cover for his operations to aid Cargill's escape - in which case those who boycotted his boats can hardly have been the other villagers as they would have known about his presbyterian connections. Robert Dick crops up again too in 1682 at Cupar where he was charged with withdrawing from the church, keeping house and field conventicles and carrying out disorderly marriages and baptisms.

Plague, invasions, witchcraft and religious persecution; the 17th century can hardly have been a settled time for those who lived at North Queensferry. Living conditions, moreover, as Stephen has explained, would have been primitive. Some homes were made of stone. More commonly they were made of wood and most were roofed with divots of turf. The floors were either flag stones or bare earth. There was no running water and dung from the houses both human and animal - for animals were often stabled on the ground floor - was piled high in the streets. Food was scarce. We have no records, but we can guess that mortality rates were high. On top of this the King was always looking for likely sailors to man His Majesty's ships. Eight were sought in Queensferry in 1626: "all to receive good pay and to be well and kindly used (!) in His Majesty's service". In 1664 Charles II was looking for "12 men out of Queensferry on both sides of the watter of Forth". Another proclamation in 1690 required 27 seamen from Inverkeithing and North Ferry. The most interesting of these Acts was one of 1672 designed to raise 500 men, giving us some idea of the relative size of North Queensferry at this time. The following numbers were required:

	Seamen
Inverkeithing	3
North Ferry	1
South Queensferry	2
Limekilns	4
Blackness	1
Leith	14
Bo'ness	6

Rosyth Castle, from an etching of 1872

Eighteenth Century Developments

The recent history of North Queensferry is
dominated by changes in transport and communication.
As far as we can tell methods of conveying people,
goods or news had changed little from mediaeval
times down to the mid seventeenth century.   From
the late 17th century onwards, however, a quickening
occurred in several related fields: new industries
sprang up; old industries began to apply fresh
methods; novel sources of motive power were
harnessed (first water, then steam); new centres
of production were set up.   Parallel innovations
occurred in farming.   All these changes implied
a need to convey raw materials, finished products
and farm produce promptly and in large quantities.
People wished to move too, to new areas where
labour was needed and employment prospects were
good.   Not only did traditional markets become
larger and more efficient, it now became possible
to supply more remote markets.   Cities grew and
rural areas suffered depopulation.   The key factor
in all this was transport.   The industrial and
agricultural revolutions of the 18th century
heralded a new pattern of life, but at the same
time they exerted a not always welcome pressure on
established patterns which stood in their way.
The transport revolution had a profound impact on
North Queensferry.

The local Ferry passage represented a long-
established monopoly, owned by landed interests
and worked by villagers.   It provided an
essential link in perhaps the most important chain
of communication in Scotland.   We have already
seen that it was not exactly the strongest link.
The ferrymen were useful according to traditional
values, but they were inefficient and their
service inadequate according to the standards of
a fast-changing society.   The days of their
lording it over the passengers were strictly
numbered.   Nevertheless the full subordination
of local to national economic interests took a
century and a half to achieve.

A book published in 1806 gives us a somewhat
idealised picture of the traditional relationship
of the village to the ferry passage: "The
inhabitants of North Queensferry have uniformly
consisted from time immemorial of operative
boatmen without any intermixture of strangers
excepting that of late a blacksmith was brought
thither by the innkeeper who is also a boatman.
They hold their homes in feu under the Marquis
of Tweedale as the successor of the Abbot of
Dunfermline.   The inhabitants of this village
have always held from generation to generation
the passage or ferry as a sort of property or
inheritance .... Nobody for ages became a
boatman or sailor on this ferry unless by
succession.   That right was always understood
by these people to be limited to the first
generation.   The children of those who had
emigrated and were born elsewhere had no
connection with this ferry; but on the other
hand, if the son of a boatman found himself
unfortunate in the world he was always entitled
to return to enter into one of the boats and take
a share of the provision which formed the estate
of the community in which he was born.   That
community has always consisted of nearly the
same number of persons.   About forty men act in
the boats .... as sailors of mature age.   The
whole community including these and the old men
and boys and the women of every age amount to
about 200 individuals.   It is kept down to
this number by emigration; because a man of
mature age usually receives no more and sometimes
less for acting as a boatman here than he could
obtain by acting as a seaman in the public service
or in that of a merchant; and he is moreover
excluded from all chance of rising in the world –
a circumstance which of itself is sufficient to
keep the number stationary.   The community has
accordingly existed for ages destitute of riches
but none of its members have been reduced to
absolute poverty or become a burden upon the
public; because by the fundamental laws of this
society the men of mature age have always
systematically laboured for the past and the
future generation and have divided with them the
bread which they earned".   This description is
based on "evidence" presented in an 18th century
legal dispute concerning the rights of working

the ferry passage. The evidence consisted of an attempt to prove the prescriptive right of the ferrymen to operate the ferry "from time immemorial". We must therefore bear in mind its possible limitations as a historical source. Nevertheless a form of mediaeval corporation of boatmen, with a collective right to work the passage is highly plausible. We know that the ferrymen thought of themselves as forming a corporation in the 17th century. Similarly a community changing little as regards numbers, status and economic role would be typical of preindustrial Scotland. Finally the idea of an exclusive community (1) with a jealously guarded source of employment comes across clearly.

A legal case in 1780 shows that the boatmen retained their reputation for incivility and unhelpfulness. Messrs Wardlaw and Anderson, merchants in Dunfermline, brought a process against James Cunningham and other tacksmen and skippers of the passage boats at Queensferry, for recovery of damages sustained upon a parcel of iron hoops made at the slit mill at Cramond for use on casks. These had been despatched in January 1776 via James Cunningham who having transported them, dumped them on the North Shore. The carter who carried the goods from Cramond asserted that he had delivered them correctly but that they had lain three nights and four days "near the place called The Hanging Stone which is much about half flood". The sea water had rusted the hoops which were now unsuitable for sale or use. In evidence it was asserted that the ferrymen had a reputation for insolence and extortion and that other ferries were more careful with goods entrusted to them. Among those who gave evidence was David Douglas, vintner of South Queensferry who ran the inn on the South side which the boatmen

(1) Consider for instance what used to be said about the Ferry town of Newport on Tay: "Take care what you say about neighbours at Newport; they are all uncles and aunties and cousins". A History of Fife and Kinross Ae. J G Mackay. Wm Blackwood and Sons. Edinburgh 1896.

used. Answers were given by "James Cunningham, Alexander McRitchie and David McRitchie all mariners in North Queensferry and tacksmen of the passage boats from North to South Queensferry". They asserted that "at the Queensferry it is the duty of the passage boatmen to convey over men and goods .... but they have no further charge of them and .... it must depend upon the state of the tides at the time whether the boat lands at one part of the shore or another". The boatmen had no time to wait and were not responsible for taking goods over the high water mark. Someone should have been sent to receive the goods. Witnesses testified that it was common to dump goods at that spot, and as the owners had been notified they should have sent for their goods sooner.

We have seen that travellers paid for the use of the ferry according to a statutory tariff. The money collected in fares or "freights" was divided in an unusual way as Forsyth describes: "On the evening of every Saturday the earnings of the week are collected into a mass: one fortieth part of the whole is deducted for the public and called "ferry silver": one fourth is set apart for the owners of the passage and the remainder is divided into shares called "deals" according to the number of persons entitled to a portion of it. One full deal is allotted to every man of mature age who has laboured during that week as a boatman whether he have acted as master or mariner or in a great boat or a yawl. Next the aged boatmen who have become unfit for labour receive half a deal or half the sum allotted to an acting boatman. Boys employed in the boats receive shares proportioned to their age from 1s 6d to a full deal or share. A small sum is also set apart for a schoolmaster and for the widows of deceased boatmen".

We can get a more precise idea of the mode of dividing the freights from Brock whose source was an undated late 18th century document now lost.

	£	s	d
Suppose the freights collected for the week were	20	-	-
Ferry silver, every 40th penny paid to the trustees for upholding the harbours and repairing the highways	-	10	-
	19	10	-
One quarter of which goes to the landed proprietors who have placed the boats on the ferry	4	17	6
	14	12	6
There are 10 widows who receive 1½d every lawful day or 9d per week	-	8	6
Schoolmaster every Saturday evening	-	2	-
	£14	2	-

"The balance (of £14-2-0) is then divided amongst the men and the boys. Every able seaman receives one deal. An old infirm seaman or any seaman who has lost a leg or arm in the service of his King and country whereby he is disabled to gain a livelihood receives half a deal and the boys are each paid a third or half a deal according to their ability to ply the passage".

Exclusive, self-sufficient and inward-looking, North Queensferry provided for its own. It is related that on one occasion a sailor named Wm Main successfully applied to the Regality Court to be registered as a ferrymen. The ferryman allowed him to work the boats for a week but on the Saturday when he came to collect his "deal" they refused to pay and bundled him out of the village. Later, however, the ferrymen took a kindlier view of two seamen who were persuaded to enlist in the Navy as representatives of the village, the ferrymen being loath to do so "for service of the passage boats". The volunteers were given a small payment and a promised that they would be "received into all the immemorial privileges of the community" on their return. After the Revolutionary War one came back to work in the boats and received a full deal; the other was "maimed" and was allotted a half deal.

The arrangements for calculating the ferry silver made in 1647 were replaced in the early 18th century by 6d in the pound "to be collected nightly and uplifted by the baillies of the Regality and the Admiralty Court of Dunfermline for the behoof of the shippings". By mid way through the century the jurisdiction of the Regality Court had been replaced by local Justices of the Peace, with whom every ferryman had to be registered. One of the last acts of the Regality Court was to raise the fares.

<u>1746 Regality of Dunfermline Revision of Fares</u>

person	2/-
horse or mare	4/-
ox or cow	4/-
highland ox or cow	3/-
sheep	4d
coach or 4 wheeled chaise	£3
two wheeled chaise	10/-
cart	12/-
horse load	3/-
express boat by night	£1-10-0

The 18th century saw several attempts to improve the landing places. That these attempts were

Illustrations : (18 marriage lintels

pretty insignificant is clear from their frequency, their inadequate funding and the fact that complaints concerning piers and landing places were as common at the end of the century as they were at its beginning. The principal source of finance for repairing the "shippings" was the ferry silver. In the late 18th century this was estimated to yield £35 annually. Even at 18th century prices such a sum was small. It was therefore supplemented by grants from other sources such as the Convention of Royal burghs. In 1762 the Convention granted £60 for repairing the shipping and harbour at North Queensferry said to be "now near completion". The next year in April a great storm damaged the "harbour and sea dykes" and again the aid of the Convention was sought. Even so, in 1769 the admiral deputes of Dunfermline asked for more funds to help them repair and amend the shippings on both sides at Queensferry. The next year the Trustees of the Forfeited Estates also gave financial assistance.

Ferry disputes

Inadequacies apart, the ferry was valuable both to those who owned it and those who worked it. Under the pressure of rapid economic change dissension grew between these parties. In the early 18th century the Laird of Dundas who had a 3/32 share in the Passage and who was therefore not entitled to put a boat on the Passage according to the 1669 regulations, put the vessel George and Allison into service. The other owners headed by the Earl of Rosebery sought an injunction to stop him. Dundas pointed out that the number of boats had risen above the number stipulated in 1669. His opponents argued that this was a reflection only of military movements of a temporary nature and that allowing his boat would, by extending the same privilege to the other proprietors, imply 11 vessels on the Passage: "It is submitted to your Lordships what havock it would make on the Passage, what Discouragement it would be to the proprietors if that business which divided amongst four boats yields a very moderate Gain were to be divided amongst eleven boats and to subsist their crews".

Worse was to come. The proprietors' share had always been burdened with the responsibility of providing boats of a specified kind and number. In the early part of the century the owners leased their one quarter share to tacksmen on whom the responsibility of supplying and maintaining boats devolved. The tacksmen paid an annual rent to the owners but in turn drew the owners' one quarter share. Out of the difference they were able to maintain the boats; any remainder they kept for themselves. The tacksmen hailed from Inverkeithing and South Queensferry and ran an association known as the boat club. Towards the end of the century the owners began to feel that their rent from letting the Passage was too small. Perhaps they felt that the boat club was getting its money too easily. Anyway in 1786 the owners failed to renew the lease with the same tacksmen as in previous years, and instead acquired their own boats and let the Passage by annual public roup to the highest bidder. The relationship between the parties under this new regime is exemplified in the following receipt: "Queensferry 25th of June 1794. Received from Messrs. Brown and Millions, now and formerly the sum of two hundred and ninety pounds sterling in full, for rent of the boats taken by them at Whitsunday one thousand seven hundred and ninety three and delivered up to me as Commissioner for the proprietors on Whitsunday one thousand seven hundred and ninety four being tacksmen of the said boats for one year."

The effect of letting the Passage by public roup was that the tacksmen had to pay a larger part of the quarter share to the proprietors. This can only have been to the financial detriment of the ferrymen. The ferry charges had been fixed in 1746 so the only way the ferrymen could maintain or improve their earnings would be from the ferry carrying more goods and passengers. Towards the end of the century during the period of Britain's war against revolutionary France, goods became scarce and prices rose. Caught between the hammer of the proprietors and the anvil of inflation the ferrymen successfully prevailed upon the proprietors to reduce their rent and therefore to leave enough income for the subsistence of ferrymen and their families. With the return of peace however in 1802, economic conditions improved. The proprietors now sought to ditch the established ferrymen and to replace them with Royal Naval personnel, suddenly in abundance following the Peace of Amiens. Forsyth describes events as follows: "they engaged a body of seamen recently dismissed from the Royal Navy under a man who had acted as master of the admiral's ship in the expedition against Holland, to navigate the boats for payment of monthly wages .... As the currents of the Frith however are at this point of headland very peculiar, it was speedily found that the seamen from the Royal Navy, however skilful in other respects, were unable to navigate the boats here. The passage boats were driven ashore sometimes above and sometimes below the proper landing places to the great terror and annoyance of the passengers. Frequently they durst not venture out in gales of wind which were despised by the native boatmen who to demonstrate their own superiority in presence of travellers who were here kept waiting, sailed backforwards and forwards with ease and safety in their own private fishing boats."

This spirited display of local skill did not keep the wolf from the door. Accordingly the ferrymen forsook their boats for the court room. Their case was compiled in the form of a "memorial" or what we might call a memorandum "from Alexander McRitchie, Alexander Jamieson, James Jamieson and James Brown, Masters of the four licensed boats upon the Passage .... for themselves and in name and behalf of the other sailors employed on the said Passage, complaines in a Bill of Suspension against the Right Honorable Neil Earl of Rosebery, Sir Robert Preston of Valleyfield Baronet, James Dundas of Dundas and his trustees, Robert Scott Moncrieff of Newhall and others styling themselves Proprietors of the Queensferry Passage, Respondents". The object was to stop the proprietors from carrying out their stratagem by obtaining a bill of suspension i.e. a legal injunction. The complaint was that the proprietors had encroached on ancient rights and privileges first established by Queen Margaret and recognised down the intervening centuries. Forsyth's account is based on this part of their memorial. A related argument was that the seamen constituted a form of corporation. The corporation had its own burying ground and mort cloth. Since 1642 it had also had a seat or loft in the church of Inverkeithing, which 20 years previous to the memorial the sailors had repaired. At the same time as the loft, a sailors' fund had been established, since managed by a succession of boxmasters and assistants. This seems to be a reference to the Sailors' Society. Deeds were produced dated 1721 and 1738 together with a new set of bye-laws dated

Inverkeithing Church

1788. Besides a prescriptive right to their work the seamen also claimed to be "a body of licensed pilots". They were quite unlike the hirelings employed to work for days wages who were strangers from Shields, Newcastle and elsewhere lately dismissed the Navy and crowded meanwhile into a single house belonging to a boatman lately dead about a quarter mile from the landing place. The memorialists were on stronger ground when they accused the proprietors of trying to quit themselves of the burden of the disabled men and widows (recipients of the "half" deal or maintenance payments out of the freights as shown above) to swell "the splendour of a few rich men of overgrown fortunes". Obviously many villagers would have to apply to the parishes of Inverkeithing and Dunfermline for support. The seamen on the other hand might be driven further away in search of work. Once gone "it will not be in the power of your Lordships to recall such a set of men from the shores of the St Lawrence or the Mississippi or to bring them back across the Alleghanny mountains if they have once lost themselves in the wilds of Kentucky". For years past "the gentlemen respondents have meditated usurpation upon the rights of the complainers". They have tried "to compare the complainers to ploughmen long employed on the same farm or colliers at the same pit. But farms and coal-pits are the absolute property of their private owners and the public has no right over them. A public ferry is of a different nature; it belongs to the public and it is at all times regulated by it. The dispute here occurs between two sets of public servants". Spirited rhetoric of this sort must have won the day, aided of course by the incompetence of the Royal Naval hirelings. Forsyth describes the predicament of the owners as follows: "Some travellers ordered post chaises and went round by Kinghorn and then threatened to prosecute these gentlemen for their expences, while others made the same threat on account of the damage suffered by the unnecessary delay of their journeys. The result was that partly from these circumstances and partly from finding that little profit was likely to arise .... and perhaps also in a considerable degree from motives of humanity, the new plan was abandoned and the inhabitants of North Queensferry restored ... to their ancient possession". Unfortunately we are not able to listen in on seamen's comments concerning the proprietors' "motives of humanity". As Brock observes "the old boatmen kept their ferry. The Napoleonic war had shaken their system. It was reserved for the coming of steam however to break it up finally".

Road improvements

The same economic pressures which led to ferry improvements, also led to road improvements. Indeed the ferry was in a sense simply a continuation of the road, so improvements in one led to improvements in the other. Before the 18th century, roads hardly merited the name: they were unsurfaced tracks, rutted in the Summer and pot-holed or swamped in the Winter. Their maintenance was in the hands of local Justices of the Peace who could compel local residents to give six days labour a year for their upkeep. The only wheeled conveyances would have been carts and waggons. Other users would have travelled on foot or horseback, sharing the way with herds of animals. We hear that in 1687 the Ferryhills road was damaged "by casting of divots, setting down of stone quarries and not allowing the just measures presented by Act of Parliament".

The break from the old system came in 1751 when Scotland's first turnpike act was passed. Under such Acts trustees were appointed. They were made responsible for repairing and maintaining a stretch of road. They were then permitted to erect toll houses and to collect tolls from those who used it. There were two toll houses near North Queensferry: one just before the motorway roundabout near what is now the main road from the village; the other, just above Jamestown. The former was demolished in 1935, the latter still stands, having recently been modernised.

Toll House, Jamestown

The turnpike road from Edinburgh to South Queensferry was begun in 1751. Only two years later, and thus one of the earliest Turnpike Acts in Scotland, we read of "an Act for repairing the road from the North Queensferry through the towns of Inverkeithing and Kinross to the town of Perth. and also the road from the said Queens Ferry to the towns of Dunfermline, Torryburn and Culross ... and also to Burntisland and Kirkcaldy". These roads are described as being "in many parts ruinous and so much out of repair that travellers cannot pass thereon without great danger". Despite this they were termed "post roads" and were described as being much used. The act appointed a large body of trustees from the neighbouring counties for "surveying, ordering, repairing and keeping in repair the said roads". It gave power to exact tolls on "any Coach, Berlin, Landau, Calash, Chaise, Chair, Waggon, Wain Cart or other carriage whatsoever or any Horse, Mare, Gelding or Mule, Ass or other cattle whatsoever". But it seemed that toll revenue would not be sufficient to keep the roads in repair so the trustees were also given power "to call out every person chargeable towards repairing and mending the roads and particularly that every householder, cottager or labourer within the said counties shall work on the highways by himself or by another employed by him for the days and under the penalties prescribed by law".

As far as we can tell, the improvements of 1753-6 affected both roads out of the village. Both of these roads were established at an early date. Stephen cites 16th century records showing a branching of the ways in the centre of the village: one road leading westwards across the shore and known as "the Kings Way to Dunfermline"; the other leading directly up the Brae northwards and known variously as the highway to Inverkeithing, the vennel or the common kirk road. An Inverkeithing Town Council minute of 1749 terms this road "the cart road leading to the Ferry". The toll house on this road above Jamestown dates from the 1753-6 improvements. Of the two roads leading from the village at this time, this seems to have been the better.

The other road leading West out of the village, followed a line lower than the present main road. It ran from the centre of the village to somewhere near Ferrybarns Farm (once situated under the approach arches of the Road Bridge but demolished during constructions of the bridge) and then turned North, still at a level below the present road. It was repaired extensively in 1756, a matter which must have been of interest to Dunfermline burgh. On July 4th 1756 the Council "after some communing anent the carrying of the turnpike road from the Ferry to this burgh, resolved that something should be done that way this season before harvest and to begin at the Spittal Bridge and carry the road on Southward", so they improved their end of the road too.

The Western route can hardly have been satisfactory. The Dunfermline Guildry records that in June 1769 trustees appointed by Act of Parliament for the turnpike road between Kinross and North Queensferry had given orders for altering the public road through the Ferryhills and that the new road proposed would go through a considerable part of the Guildry's lands of the Ferryhills. Three years later the damage caused by this new road to the Guildry's lands was assessed at £32-10-0. In 1778 Robert Millions claimed damages "as per tack for the new turnpike road leading thro' his possessions

for five years".   This seems to imply that by
1773 the line of the new road was complete,
particularly as in that year the Guildry had
recorded that "the old road leading through the
Guildry's haugh at the ferry to the haugh well is
now agreed to be deserted as a public road" ....
and "now only used as a road to ye haugh well".
The Haugh refers to the shallow hollow of ground

In May 1765 a coach started the run from Edinburgh
to Newhalls (The Hawes Inn, South Queensferry).
Each passenger paid two shillings.   The coach ran
twice a day in Summer and once a day in Winter.
On the North side the coach ran every Tuesday and
Friday to Perth, and in the other direction every
Monday and Thursday starting from Perth at 7 a.m.
The fare from Perth to North Queensferry was 7/6d.

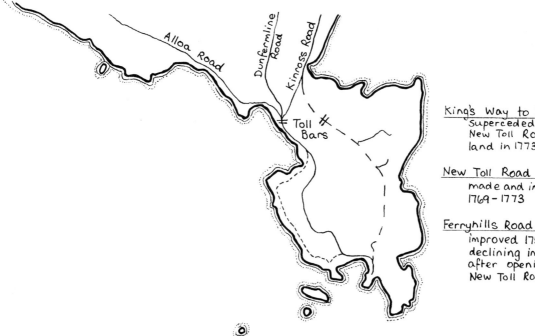

King's Way to Dunfermline
    Superceded by
    New Toll Road, on higher
    land in 1773

New Toll Road
    made and improved in
    1769 - 1773

Ferryhills Road
    improved 1753-1756 but
    declining in importance
    after opening of
    New Toll Road.

on the East of the Road Bridge which is skirted by
the present main road and on part of which Inchcolm
Drive now stands.   The Guildry applied to the
Justices of the Peace to shut this road.   In lieu
they applied for access "by the present road to
the White Dyke and down from that in a straight
line south to the well".   In the same year the
Guildry also considered "repairing the Easter
shippings and roads leading thereto".

Thus in the last quarter of the 18th century there
were two routes northwards from the ferry: the
old road which now declined in importance and which
by the turn of the century had ceased to exist as
a highway (Stephen) and the new road built in
1769-73.   The route superseded by the new road
nevertheless appears on maps in the late 18th and
early 19th centuries, although by then it can
hardly have been more than a track.   At the Ferry
Toll this track joined with the new road; at the
other end it had been closed by the Guildry as
described above.

Improved roads set the scene for the early coaching
era.   In 1786 the 60 hour coach was established
between London and Edinburgh.   It depended upon
22 separate teams of horses and was miraculously
fast.   "Stories were told of men and women who
having reached London with such celerity, died
suddenly of an affection of the brain".   The
speeds, which varied between 7 and 10 mph, can
hardly have endangered life, but bumpy roads, poor
springs and collisions were hazards.   In 1791
such considerations prompted the Postmaster
General to warn not to send cash by post because of
the "friction it occasions from the great
expedition with which it is conveyed".

This coach described in 1775 as "a board above
the axle of a pair of wheels drawn by a single
horse" carried a single passenger and the mail.
The 30 mile journey took 14 hours.   In that year
a new coach "The Fly" was introduced on the same
route.   It ran three times a week from the
Salutation Hotel, Perth at the same speed but was
drawn by two horses and carried four passengers.
In 1787 James Skelton proprietor of the Green Inn
Kinross began a coach service to North Queensferry.

Thus by the end of the 18th century several
coaches were running to North Queensferry carrying
passengers, mail and other articles.

Travellers' reactions

What did travellers make of the Ferry and the
village at this time?   Reverend Wm MacRitchie
Minister of Clunie, Perthshire arrived at North
Queensferry with his horse, Cally, and wrote
"Breakfast at the Ferry.   No prospect of a passage
till afternoon;   contrary winds and heavy rains ...
have a quick rough passage of nine minutes along
with some of the King's Black Horse (Major Watson).
Arrive in Edinburgh in the evening".   Dr Johnson
crossed the Forth further down river and so perhaps
fortunately, was unable to pronounce on the village.
Boswell remarked that the view across the water
was "after Constantinople and Naples, the finest
prospect in Europe", evoking a characteristic
reply from Johnson: "Water is the same everywhere".
In 1792 Robert Heron travelled to Perth on the
Edinburgh to Aberdeen "stage coach or rather chaise".
He found the inn at South Queensferry "not more
than tolerable".   On the passage boat he met
carriers and reapers from the Highlands.   He left

North Queensferry by "a winding, rising road".
Alexander Campbell coming in the opposite direction
noted the new road to the ferry took to the right.
On the other hand "the road which formerly led
to the North Ferry from Inverkeithing was conducted
over the hill with as little regard to convenience
as to the ease and comfort of travellers. A new
line however, much better planned has removed the
inconveniences complained of, but the new route
has lost "the grand and sublime prospects" of the
old. He advises the traveller on foot or on
horseback to go that way and "if driving, to quit
his equipage and send it round by the new road".
Quite clearly the old road referred to here is the
Easterly route, still known as the old road but
now much altered, the middle section having been
re-routed after a recent quarry extension.

The Old Statistical Account was compiled by parish
ministers all over Scotland in the 1790's. Rev.
Andrew Robertson wrote the entry for Inverkeithing.
He notes that the population of North Queensferry
was 312 people and that "all the boatmen reside
in the North Ferry. There are four boats and
four yawls .... the common freight is far too low
being only a penny each passenger ...this passage
is safe and expeditious. Passage may be had at all
times excepting .... high winds together with
particular and unfavourable times of the tide.
There was a large boat overset some years ago by
a sudden squall and its being fully loaded with
black cattle, the boatmen were lost and also the
passengers". Alexander Campbell must have read
this report for he advises "when the boats are
loaded with black cattle passengers ought to avoid
them lest any sudden squall should upset them and
endanger their lives".

Rev J. Henderson the minister for South Queensferry
noted that since the Ferry Passage had been let by
public roup the travelling public had made several
gains. The boats were in excellent repair.
Regulations of the passage were painted on boards
"and affixed at some proper place on the inns at
both sides". In addition there were two
arbitrators, one on either side to decide in cases
of dispute concerning fares or other ferry
regulations. Nevertheless the landing places
were still exceptionally bad and passengers on the
South side "have to scramble a considerable way
among rocks and large stones rendered slippery by
being covered with wet sea weed". The fund for
repairing these landing places (the ferry silver)
amounted to an average of £35 per annum "a sum
far from sufficient".

Finally George Combe, later well-known in Edinburgh
as a phrenologist came to South Queensferry as a
boy in 1796. He seems not to have enjoyed his
stay which was in the nature of a convalescence.
However on one occasion he made the crossing
on the ferry boat."My joy was great for I had a
passion for sailing and had never before been
afloat. A soft west wind wafted us across, all
too soon for me, but it was a day of exciting
adventure. We went to the inn and had a bottle
of nice ale and some sea biscuits. I rambled
about the village and trod on ground on which I had
cast many a longing look from the other side of
the Firth and returned considering myself a
travelled youth".

Military preparations

Compared with the 17th century, the 18th was a
peaceful time for the people of North Queensferry.
Nevertheless the growth of British maritime power
which culminated in the Battle of Trafalgar implied
a need for able-bodied seamen, and it was
convenient to obtain them from ports and coastal
towns, if necessary by force. Stephen notes
that the Press Gang operated in Inverkeithing and
at one stage paraded the town during an election
armed with swords and pistols to give support to
a naval candidate. In 1758 the Inverkeithing
Council disbursed £7-5-0 Scots for "furnishings to
the pressed men" and in 1793 when war was declared
against revolutionary France the Inverkeithing
Sailors Society reported that "a house of
rendezvous has been opened and a press gang
established in this town which has of late committed
several illegal and oppressive acts of violence
unprecedented on the inhabitants and neighbourhood".
Press gangs were feared by seamen and their
families. David Wilson a Fife fisherman returning
from a whaling trip to Greenland aboard "The Advice"
found the homeward trip intercepted by the warship
"Pickle". He and his friends captured their own
captain and officers and sought to turn their ship
to safety, but "Pickle" turned its guns on "The
Advice" and boarded her. Wilson was put below with
a six foot iron bar across his legs and his hands
fixed to ring bolts. He was acquitted by a London
Court of mutiny but was returned to naval service
in "Pickle".

*Sketch from an early print:
"Loading cattle at Kyleakin"*

The Queensferry passage was an essential service
so the Ferrymen were "not liable to be impressed"
in Brock's felicitous phrase. They were protected
from the press gangs in the war of the Austrian
Succession and later during the war against
revolutionary France. We have seen that in this
war they persuaded two outsiders to do naval
service in their stead in return for the privilege
of becoming ferrymen on their return from the war.
This implies that not all of them were exempt from
naval duties. In 1793 for instance Francis
Freeling later Secretary of the Post Office had to
take urgent action to prevent 12 boatmen from being
pressed into the navy.

During the American War of Independence, Paul Jones
an American privateer entered the Forth with a

squadron of French ships intent on plundering the coastal towns. Luckily adverse weather turned him back. The lesson of 1779 was nevertheless quickly learned. Coastal repairs and fortifications were begun, notably at Leith where a fort was constructed. In June 1781 a delegation from the Dunfermline Guildry, which owned Castlehill, (the projecting land virtually under the present Railway Bridge on which a battery had stood at the time of the Cromwellian invasion) met Captain Fraser, chief army engineer for Scotland, "to settle with him a battery to be built on the point of the Ness". On behalf of the Government, Captain Fraser asked for temporary use of the land, to which the Guildry agreed, provided their tenant was indemnified against any resultant loss and on condition that any buildings constructed would revert to them. But if the ground were needed any longer than the present war, (The War of American Independence) the Government was to purchase it. In 1782 American Independence was recognised but now a war with France looked possible,so once more a delegation was sent down to Queensferry, this time to meet Mr Thomas Fyres "overseer of His Majesty's Works" as well as Fraser. They "perambulated" Castlehill and the East Ness which was found to measure 7 acres, 2 roods and 8 falls. The Guildry thereupon suggested a price but Andrew Fraser (now promoted to Major) demonstrated how wise the army had been to promote him by declining to purchase. He suggested "some annual acknowledgement". The Guildry tried to invoke the earlier agreement without success but agreed to the Government occupying the land a year or two longer on the former terms. Subsequently two forts were built, "a higher and a lower battery mounting together eight iron guns, twenty pounders and eight field pieces". (Old Statistical Account)

Another aspect of the war, the billeting of troops seems not to have greatly bothered the village, although in 1800 South Queensferry complained that "withe these twelve months upwards of 82000 cavalry and infantry besides women and children have been quartered in this place and neighbourhood when they might easily have stopped at North Queensferry or Inverkeithing .... places of larger or more convenience seldom or never get them". This was something less than a fraternal suggestion from our brothers across the water.

Another product of the war was the volunteer movement. Participants, known as "fencibles", were in effect forerunners of the Home Guard. Partly from reasons of patriotism, partly perhaps to avoid more distant active service, the boatmen offered their services in defence of their country. In 1797 thirty two boatmen and inhabitants of North Queensferry offered their services to the Lord Provost of Edinburgh in these terms: "We His Majesty's loyal subjects, inhabitants and seamen of North Queensferry having been informed that our enemies threaten an actual invasion of Great Britain .... make a tender of our services in defence of our King and Country and the British Constitution at the battery of Inch Garvie, North Ferry and Island Colm if required .... Signed this third day of March 1797". The letter was signed by those offering their services and is thought to have been penned by Mr Inglis the schoolmaster. Amongst the signatures the name Brown appears five times, a name which was wide-spread in the village in former times. (In 1802 families bearing the name of Brown possessed about one half of the sailors' burial ground.) The

Lord Provost passed the letter to Lord Adam Gordon, Commander of the Forces. The latter presented his compliments to the Lord Provost and asked him to thank the boatmen for their offer "which does them much honour and shall be published in the newspapers accordingly". We also have a record, a few years later of the Kings Commission of James Brown as First Lieutenant of the North Queensferry Volunteer Artillery:

"We George the Third by the Grace of God of the United Kingdom of Great Britain and Ireland, King, Defender of the Faith, &c, to our Trusty and Welbeloved James Brown, Greeting. We do by these Presents Constitute and Appoint you to be First Lieutenant of the North Queensferry Volunteer Artillery commanded by Our Trusted and Welbeloved Captain Munro Ross, but not to take rank in Our Army except during the time of the said corps being called out into actual service. You are therefore carefully and diligently to Discharge the duty of First Lieutenant by Exercising and Well disciplining both the inferior Officers and Soldiers of that Company and We do, hereby, Command them to Obey you as their First Lieutenant, and You are to observe and follow such Orders and Directions, from Time to Time, as you shall receive from your Captain or any other your Superior Officers, according to the Rules and Discipline of War, in pursuance of the Trust hereby reposed in You. Given at our Court at Saint James's the Twenty fifth day of June 1803, in the Forty Third Year of Our Reign", &c &c In handwriting: "James Brown Gent, 1st Lieut of the North Queensferry Volunt. Artillery".

Seal of the Dunfermline Guildry
(Actual size)

CHAPTER V

Ferry Improvements

On 31st October 1807, a general meeting of the
"Trustees upon the Queensferry and Perth Turnpike
Road" was held at Kinross.   William Adam, the
prime mover in subsequent road and ferry
improvements, presented a "memorial" to the
meeting.   He was proprietor of Blair Adam,
Lord Lieutenant of the County of Kinross, and an
influential representative of enlightened
commercial and landed interests on the North side
of the crossing.   He noted the importance of
the Great North Road which gave access to Perth
and beyond, and of the water passage, "the most
resorted to of any in the kingdom" but drew
attention to certain defects in them.   He
argued that private owners of the ferry, however
well-intentioned, could not attend adequately to
the needs of the travelling public;   that the
local Justices of the Peace were not armed with
sufficient powers for regulating the ferry;   that
the shipping places were ill-contrived;   that
keeping the passage boats on the North side often
detained travellers coming from the South;   and
that the absence of alternative piers (there
were only three: one on the North and two on the
South side) prevented the boats from sailing in
adverse conditions.   He pointed out that the
Passage was used by stage and mail coaches going
as far as Aberdeen and that it was militarily as
well as commercially important.   He then unfolded
plans for its improvement.

The crux of the plan was an Act of Parliament
whereby the ferry would be taken into public
ownership and administered by trustees.   The
idea was to seek government aid for half the cost
of the improvements and to raise the rest by
private subscription.   With the funds, old
landing places would be repaired and new ones
built to permit a number of alternative diagonal
crossings, which would eliminate unnecessary
tacking and permit sailings irrespective of wind
or tide;   berths would be built on the South
side;   and new rules would be introduced for
running the ferry.   Those present were clearly
impressed by Adam's suggestions.   They accepted
his memorial, appointed a large steering committee
and resolved to seek an Act of Parliament to

implement the proposed changes.

In July 1808 a general meeting of the "Trustees
for improving the landing places on both sides
of the water at Queensferry" was held "within
Mitchell"s Inn" (fore runner of the Albert Hotel).
Recent moves were reported, and the meeting gave
a favourable response to the proposed improvements,
provided that half of the funds could be raised
from the Government.   At another meeting held
at Kinross in November, Mr Adam reported a meeting
with the Chancellor of the Exchequer.   It was
resolved to press for an Act of Parliament the
next year, and therefore a London committee and a
London solicitor were appointed.   The trustees
thereupon recorded their gratitude to Mr Adam.

These moves had been followed closely by the
proprietors of the Queensferry Passage.
Accordingly in December 1808 they met to defend
their property.   Present at the meeting which
took place in Edinburgh were the Rt Hon Lord
Viscount Primrose, Earl of Rosebery, Robert
Scott Moncrieff of Newhalls, Mathew Wilkie of
Bonnington, James Thomson WS for Sir Robert
Preston of Valleyfield and John Dundas WS for
James Dundas of Dundas.   Unlike the reformers,
most of the proprietors were from the South
side (although Scott Moncrieff and Preston owned
land on Ferryhills).   They resolved to oppose
the Bill, but nevertheless approved the proposal
for new berthing facilities for ferry boats at
Newhalls.   They objected to everything else,
especially to the wide powers claimed by the new
trustees to build roads, piers and buildings "to
the irreparable injury of the very proprietors
whose ground they are to have a warrant for
thus seizing".   Their horror at the "violent
invasions of private property" was second only
to their fear that any resultant compensation
might err on the low side.   They argued that
compensation should be based not on the ferry
revenues of the previous twenty years as
proposed, but on the future revenues after
improvement.   Their prospective loss could
"scarcely be estimated by any pecuniary equivalent".

Following this meeting Lord Viscount Primrose addressed Wm Adam in a letter larded with ingratiation, in which greater apprehension was expressed for the future of the Earl of Rosebery's "residence with ornamented grounds" than for the convenience of the travelling public. Wm Adam accepted the Viscount's "kind personal expressions" and assured him that "feelings on that score are perfectly reciprocal". He continued "I am confident that my regard and esteem for your Lordship is founded on what cannot be disturbed by a difference, however fundamental, on a subject of public regulation". He insisted on the need for the powers claimed in the Bill and concluded that the issue reduced to "the mere question of compensation".

the town pier was to be lengthened and improved; a new pier was to be built between Long Craig and the shore; boatmen's houses and a superintendent's house were to be built, likewise an inn on the lands belonging to the Guildry.

All these alterations were estimated to cost £18,500, half of which was to be met by the Exchequer, the other half by private subscription. Subscriptions were sought from "persons of fortune and distinction" in the locality. Each was to pay £500 to be secured on the annual produce of the ferry. In the meantime three people gave their names as security to obtain a bank loan of £10,000. This was matched by an advance from the Exchequer of the same amount, which provided enough funds to purchase the ferry and to

The Albert Hotel

formerly
Mitchell's Inn

The reformers now petititioned the House of Commons for a Bill. The ferry was described as the chief communication between North and South Scotland, and the principal military communication. In the previous half year 1300 carriages had paid the post horse duty at the ferry. Besides the mail coach, stage coach and gentlemen's carriages,thousands of cattle had crossed. The petition dwelt on the defects: crossings being effectively limited to nine out of every twenty four hours; the lack of transit at low water; the dangerous landing places; insubordination of the ferrymen; and the inconvenience to the ferries resulting from other traffic using wharves and creeks. As we shall see the latter point was keenly contested by local residents but was decided against them. As for the ferry proprietors, they came out of it quite well. They eventually agreed to sell their interests in the ferry for £8673-13-10½d and obtained legal assurances concerning public encroachment on their lands.

John Rennie was employed to survey the ferry passage and to make recommendations. His proposals were shown in a "Plan of the Frith of Forth with the improvements at Queensferry and Landing Places published by order of the trustees, 1810" and embodied in a schedule to the Act of Parliament. On the South side there were to be: a pier at Long Craig, East of Newhalls, with an access road to Newhalls; a longer pier at Newhalls; a new pier at Port Edgar with a new access road; and houses for a superintendent and boatmen. In deference to the ex owners of the ferry, no inn was planned and the road from Long Craig to Newhalls, was to be restricted in width and walled on one side. On the North side the East Battery landing place and the road leading to it were to be improved; a new landing place was to be built West of the Battery;

start construction. The list of original trustees of the Queensferry Passage looks like an invitation list to the Queen's garden party:
   Keeper of the Great Seal of Scotland
   Keeper of the Privy Seal of Scotland
   Lord Justice General
   Lord Advocate
   Lord Justice Clerk
   Lord Clerk Register
   Lord Chief Baron of Exchequer
   Vice Admiral of Scotland
   Keeper of HM Signet
   Postmaster General of Scotland
   HM Lieutenants of the Counties of
     Perth, Linlithgow, Fife, Kinross
     and Clackmannan
   Admiral Commanding HM Ships in the
     Firth of Forth
   Lord Provost of Edinburgh
   Chief Magistrates of Perth, Linlithgow,
     Queensferry, Inverkeithing and
     Dunfermline
   Sheriffs depute of the above counties
   Proprietor of New Halls and everyone
     in the above counties possessed of
     lands valued at £200 or more in the
     cess books (and the eldest sons of
     such persons)

The trustees were empowered to raise loans on the security of the tolls, to make rules and byelaws for the good government of the ferry, to acquire land, and to undertake construction in the places shown on the plans and to make and maintain roads. But "it shall not be lawful to make or use any road or path upon the sea shore towards Edinburgh .... save and except the public roads and paths now in use and the roads described in the schedule". It became unlawful for anyone to

dispose of ballast, rubbish, ashes or dust in any
of the ferry harbours or within 600 ft of any
pier; or to obstruct or interrupt the ferry.
The trustees were to appoint 15 of their members
as a committee of management but the government
finally appointed eight including Lord Elgin, Lord
Colville of Culross, and Lord Dunfermline.
Finally the practice of putting the ferry out to
auction was to continue. One of the boatmen
would act as tacksman and thus the old arrangements
for providing for the schoolmaster and for the
widows of boatmen continued.

The trustees assumed responsibility for the ferry
on 10th May 1810 with the aim of rendering the
ferry "as perfect for transit by sailing boats as
the nature of the thing would admit". By 1812
the total cost of improving the Great North Road
and the ferry and of purchasing ownership of
ferry had risen to £27,050. Half of the money
was provided initially by the British Linen Bank;
the other half by the government. The first
half was to be replaced with £500 bonds to be
held by members of the public. The arrangement
was said to demonstrate "the benefit which results
from the interposition of trustees of rank and
consideration when it is reserved for objects
of sufficient magnitude".

The first phase of work saw the construction of
Long Craig pier on the South side and East Battery
pier on the North. In addition on the North side
the West Battery and Town piers were improved and
extended. Communicating roads were built as
were boatmen's homes, a signal house and light
houses. A superintendent's house was purchased
on the North side and James Scott "perfectly
accustomed to the habits of command and skilled
in the navigation and management of the vessels"
was appointed superintendent. All the boats on
the ferry were repaired and five new ones built.
Finally the trustees set down regulations for
the passage. Copies were displayed in the inns
on either side and were carried in the pocket of
each skipper. In the event of serious complaint
the trustees held a Justice of the Peace court
every Monday.

Captain Scott's Seabank Cottage

After the first stage of construction the trustees
had made the following disbursements:

North side

£4206-19-6 Building from the
foundation new pier at the Battery
on the North side, on which is
erected a home for boatmen to wait
in and a shed for the shelter of foot
passengers together with a road of
communication from this pier to the
turnpike road the greatest part of
which it was necessary to cut thro'
solid rock.

£406-10-0 A signal house which
contains on the ground floor a room
for the boat crews in waiting, a room
for the accommodation of the
superintendent and for transacting
the justice business connected with
the passage (answering at the same
time the purpose of a light house).

£260-9-1 Residence for the
superintendent with a small garden
attached - from which he has a
complete view of the Passage.

£300 Purchase of a strip of land
leading from the turnpike to the
shore opposite Long Craig.

£206-15-6 Improving the quay at
North Ferry by filling up the angle
on the North East side of the quay.

South side

£4763-13-0 Port Edgar pier.

£8096-00-0 Newhalls pier. Spacious
pier with a breakwater in the centre
and a paved road on each side
"rendering the accommodation for
boating and un-boating carriages easy
and convenient".

£587-11-11 A small pier blasted out
of the rock East of Newhalls.

£909-11-6 Land and building of six
boatmen's houses.

£500-00-0 Purchase of new boats and
pinnaces.

£1281-1-1 Initial expenses.

£8673-13-10½ Purchase of ferry.

Total expenditure £30,792-6-3½, of which
contributed by Barons of HM Exchequer
in Scotland - £13,586-11-8d.

This list excludes some expenditures on the Great
North Road. Allowing for these, by this stage, the
trustees had spent a third more than had been
envisaged initially, but had still not implemented the
whole of the original plan. The principal omission
was the Long Craig Pier on the North side which had
been considered crucial to the plan. It would have
allowed a crossing between here and Port Edgar
at all times of tide and wind. Besides it would

have relieved the inconvenience of "eddy tides and baffling winds created by the island of Inch Garvie" in crossing to Newhalls. Unforeseen expenses, however, included expenses on the turnpike near Newhalls and work on the lighthouse and superintendent's house on the South side. Besides there had been extra expense in cutting rock, sinking sinking rock beneath the sea and employing artificers. All in all the trustees estimated they would need another £20,000 to complete the job, a sum which was not then available. Long Craig pier on the North side was never built. Nevertheless Duncan's Itinerary (1823) shows a causeway out to Long Craig and the pier as if it had been completed. "Proposed new inn and offices" on Scotts Brae are also shown. As for the rest of the ferry improvements, it seems ironic that so much was spent on creating conditions which would enable sailing ships to make diagonal crossings, at the very moment when the advent of steam would make such crossings unnecessary.

Guildry's harbour. As Captain M'Konochie later observed, the ferry improvers had taken "forcible possession of the whole sea-front, pier and all "so that the village baker is unable to land his wheat, the mason his lime, the carpenter his wood". The result was the "virtual disfranchisement of an unoffending population of 500 souls and their exclusion from the exercise of the most natural right which can belong to a seafaring community, the right of communicating with the element on which they earn their bread". Obviously the villagers' extremity had been the Guildry's opportunity. We do not know exactly where their pier was located. M'Konochie speaks of a pier recently begun about the middle of North Queensferry harbour, ie on the East side of the village off Battery Road. There are remains of what could have been a short pier at this point. This was not a ferry pier and as the Guildry had owned neighbouring Castlehill until selling it to the military, this may well have been the

Hawes Inn at Newhalls,
South Queensferry

Incomplete the ferry may have been; it was nevertheless a thing of some beauty. William Adam was proud to announce that in the year to 15th May 1811 an average of 228 persons had made the crossing per day. During the year insurable property valued at almost £1M had been carried. Other crossings were as follows:

carriages	1,515
carts	4,254
horses	13,154
cattle	18,057
sheep	25,151
barrel bulk	5,520
dogs	2,615

Comparing these figures with those for the Tay ferry in 1824, less foot passengers used the Queensferry but for all other categories the Queensferry was far superior - carrying 60% more sheep, more than twice as many cattle - and this, 13 years earlier with its ferry improvements barely complete. Campbell who toured Scotland in 1811 refers to 4 ferry boats and 4 yawls carrying up to a maximum of 450 passengers daily.

A humble request

In the eye of local residents however the improvements were viewed differently. In 1811 "the inhabitants and fishers of North Queensferry" complained to the Guildry of Dunfermline about the charges levied by James Brown, tacksman at the

pier referred to.

The complaint of the villagers was that the charges for using the Guildry pier were too high. The charge of 6d per boat for entering the harbour was "unreasonable and oppressive" and the weekly charge of 2/- "most ridiculous". Similarly a charge of 6d was too high for a carter who wished to purchase fish. They suggested that the charges be 1/6d per week, or 3d a day per boat or per cart. Even at these levels "we think that said tacksmen will be at no disadvantage to make your honours' rent and something handsome for his trouble". Unless charges were reduced, the villagers felt that there would be "less occupying of said harbour particularly by strange boats". They ended their letter respectfully as they had begun it "The above is humbly submitted to your honours' due consideration and remain Gentlemen, your honours' humble and Obedt. servs. Gentlemen we will take it as a condescending favour to have your honours' answer to the above so as it may be the means of preventing any disturbance or feuding with Mr Brown tacksman about the matter"

William Anderson
William Blaik
John Davie

The middle class steamship

The improvements at Queensferry were obsolete almost before they were complete. The steam-powered "Charlotte Dundas" was running on the Forth Clyde canal in 1802. Ten years later a passenger steamer, "The Comet", ran at a speed of 5 knots on the Clyde. Very soon, steam boats appeared on the Forth running between Leith, Grangemouth, Kincardine, Alloa and Stirling. They attracted both trippers and genuine travellers, so that there was a perceptible drop in Queensferry passengers and an increase in those using the Broad Ferry (Newhaven-Burntisland). Clearly with such a challenge the trustees would have to act quickly.

Estuary of the Forth

At most other ports, passengers were carried to and from the steamships, which remained in deep water. This was called floorying. "But in the narrow strait of Queensferry, where from ten to fifteen minutes is the ordinary length of passage, to embark and disembark four times in order to get steam for the short middle passage would be worse than making the whole transit by sailing boat". The solution would be for the steamboat to come alongside the quays. But their gradient had been determined for sailing ships, and this created a difficulty. The trustees' first step was to hire the steamship "Lady of the Lake". She was contracted at £6 per day from the 1st January 1821 and subjected to intensive trials. The results were favourable, the advantages of using her for towing the sailing boats in light North West winds being apparent to all the ferrymen. Superintendent Scott was equally impressed. He agreed that the quays were unsuitable for a steamboat of great power and dimension. On the other hand a small boat would not be able to cope with the tides and winds while towing other vessels. He therefore recommended a "middle class steam boat" with suggested dimensions as follows:

    7½ feet from keel to gunnel
    60 feet from stern to stern
    17½ feet beam
    16 horsepower engine weighing 22 tons
    shallow hold carrying 60 tons
    total cost £1,900

The estimated weekly expense of a steamship of this sort was given as:

	£	s	d
Engineer	1	10	-
Skipper	1	5	-
2 Seamen	1	16	-
Fireman	-	17	-
Coals	5	10	-
Tallow, oil, rope, yarns	1	16	-
	£12	14	-

Set against this was a cost saving of £11-10-6 because the steamship would allow the trustees to do away with one boat crew and two pinnace crews. Taking into account certain additional unbudgeted expenses of the steamboat (maintaining machinery, painting, cleaning and caulking) and allowing for attracting 20,000 more passengers at increased freights, there might be an overall surplus of £150 for the year - sufficient to pension off 4 infirm ferrymen at 1/- per day (such men to make themselves useful on the pier when they are able) and to give the tacksmen an increased income of £77.

These forecasts were accepted and the steamship "Queen Margaret" was the result. Captain Scott made a model of the new ship on a scale ½" to the foot. The new ship was built to his specification, but not to his original estimate. The eventual cost was £2,369 with the money being found by pledging the Trust's sinking fund. The new boat was a success but not an unqualified one. She failed to bring back to Queensferry the foot and coach passengers which had been lost to the Broad Ferry. Moreover in use, her draught increased by six inches making it difficult to approach the piers at all tides. Captain Scott's remedy was to increase her length by 10 feet. This adjustment gave her a better speed and raised her 8-10 inches in the water. The "Queen Margaret" was launched on October 1st 1821 and the day was commemorated with a meeting of the trustees at Newhalls Inn. They reported that at that stage the following sums had been spent on the improvements:

    £19,220 advanced by Parliament

    £16,819-14-4 advanced by private
                 interests

These sums were secured on the revenue of the ferry. The rent paid by the tacksmen at this time was £1,800 per annum, a reduction of some £500 on its level before the Broad Ferry had begun to steal the traffic. Apart from the "Queen Margaret" the trustees had the following

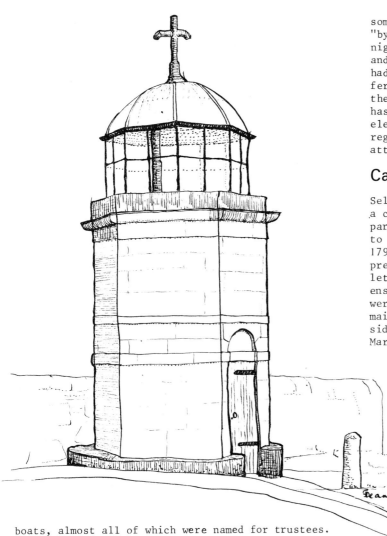

Lighthouse at Signal House Pier, North Queensferry. '77

some of them living on the South side, and also "by the establishment of watchmen during the night, of light-houses, of signals during fogs, and of beacons on the rocks". No accidents had occurred to a single passenger since the ferry had been vested in trustees. They gave their thanks "To Mr Scott of the Royal Navy who has been superintendent of the Passage for eleven years past and who has managed the regulation of the ferry with great judgement attention and prudence".

Carrying the night mails

Self congratulation apart, the Queensferry was a constant source of delay and inconvenience, particularly for the Post Office in its efforts to achieve a more efficient mail service. In 1796, the Post Office surveyor, Ronaldson, was present at South Queensferry when the ferry was let by contract for the year. He wished to ensure that the boatmen who obtained the contract were aware of their obligation to carry the mails. In the meantime the boatmen on the North side demanded more pay. No sooner was "Queen Margaret" in service than the Post Office decided

boats, almost all of which were named for trustees.

Boats

Prince Regent	(Head of the armed forces during the Napoleonic War)
Blair Adam	(Home of Wm Adam)
Primrose	(Family name of the Roseberys)
Earl of Moray	(Also a trustee)

Pinnaces

Pitfirrane	(Sir Charles Halkett, a trustee from Pitfirrane)
Dunearn	(James Stuart, convener of the Committee of Management from Dunearn)
Keavil	(Dr James Robertson Barclay, another trustee, from Keavil)

Yawls

| (unnamed) | (There were three of these to be used in calm weather) |

The trustees noted that the ferry had attracted very few complaints, the boatmen being "generally sober, orderly and industrious men". The regulation of the ferry had been much improved by

it wanted to send the mail at night instead of during the day. The aim was to speed up the service. Previously the mails had crossed at first light. William Adam was aware of the vulnerability of the ferry finances and was quick to call a meeting of the trustees at his house in George Street, Edinburgh. He explained to the meeting that the ferry dues were let to the principal boatmen in return for their services working the ferry and maintaining the boats, but that many of the expenses of running the ferry devolved upon the trustees: items such as the maintenance of lighthouses and piers, and the salary of the superintendent. The trustees also had to pay interest on each £500 bond taken by private investors. He indicated that competition for traffic had diminished the ferry takings and had resulted in a reduction of rent paid by the tacksmen. Thus there was a danger that the Post Office proposal would constitute a further drain on resources: there would be extra expenses of fuel and in wages paid to crews besides the risks of navigation at night.

Captain Scott also wrote a memorandum. He pointed out that "In gales or squally weather the gusts are sudden owing to this strait being nearly surrounded with high land. In the day time even when every eye is on watch ... accidents can only be prevented by seeing such a gust take the water and preparing to receive it".

He doubted the safety of navigating the passage "under cloud of night". He also estimated the cost of carrying the night mail as £200 per annum by "half-tide decked boat" and £744 per annum by steamer. The trustees felt there were two main alternatives - either the Post Office should buy its own boat and man it or it should negotiate an annual sum to be paid to the trustees in order that the trustees carry out the function. A series of meetings were convened by the trustees at various Edinburgh hotels. At the Waterloo Hotel in early December 1821 the following figures were said to be typical:

	£	£
Average years rent		1,800
Repair of piers	150	
Boat repairs and replacements	150	
Lighting	50	
Salaries and wages	350	
Incidental expenses	50	
Interest on bonds	840	
Surplus		210

The surplus was thought to be quite modest in view of the need to set up a sinking fund to repay the bonds and to replace the steamship at some future date. The trustees nevertheless resolved that it was incumbent on them to provide a fast, regular and safe conveyance of the mail at whatever time might be expedient for the Post Office. That duty was only limited by impractibility or inadequacy of funds. Ultimately, the result of skilful lobbying was that the Treasury offered to pay the trustees £200 per annum if they carried the night mails. The arrangement would work for the first 3 years with a review thereafter. The trustees agreed to this proposal, no doubt relieved to get government assistance. Later the contract between the trustees and the Post Office survived suggestions by both the Broad Ferry and the Kirkcaldy Chamber of Commerce that the mail crossing should be made further down river.

Regulations

From Duncan's Itinerary of Scotland (published Glasgow, 1823) we get a detailed account of the ferry regulations and charges at this time. One boat, one pinnace and one yawl were to be kept on the South side where at least 8 boatmen were to reside. Each boat was to be navigated by at least 5 men (or 4 men and a boy). the pinnaces and yawls had a complement of 4 men (or 2 men and 2 boys). In stormy weather the Superintendent was to appoint crews as he thought fit. The boatmen were not to receive money other than that authorised by the regulations. Carts were to be weighed on a weighing machine on the North side and charged according to the table of freights. The boats and pinnaces were not to be freighted to the exclusion of other passengers but yawls could be. Passengers, horse or carriages were not to be conveyed in the same boat with cattle unless with consent. In addition passengers were to have priority over carts and cattle. The regulations regarding porters were displayed on the vessels, but unfortunately no record exists concerning

their contents. Finally the superintendent at North Queensferry was "at all times to hold himself in readiness to give attendance to passengers with full power to enforce the freights and regulations".

The regulations for the "Queen Margaret" were given separately. She was to sail hourly and half hourly unless replaced by a boat or pinnace by authority of the Superintendent. The passenger freight by steamboat or by a boat towed by her was 6d and half price for children. Cattle above 40 stone weight were carried at 8d each. "Queen Margaret" could be chartered "at times not convenient for the general purposes of the ferry" at a charge of 7/6d. She was not to run on Sundays. Here is the full table of freights:

Table of freights

7/6	coach, barouche, or landau
10/-	hearse
1/-	horse
6d	mule or ass
5d	ox, bull, cow or heifer
3d	calf, sow or boar
1d	lamb or kid
1d	dog or puppy
6d	passengers
3d	children under 12
Free	mail horses or expressed from the Post Office
"	soldiers on march
"	horses of officers
"	ordnance carts
"	volunteers in uniform
"	carts carrying vagrants with legal passes

Large boat	Hire of boat
5/-	2/6 in daylight
6/-	5/- in dark

More criticisms : more improvements

No service however well planned and executed, runs perfectly. In his "Memorial" to the trustees Captain Scott admitted that his boats did not always run on time. This was particularly the case with the large boats. These boats which were meant to sail each hour accomplished 14-15 sailings per day from each shore. Two boats and two crews had difficulty in managing so many crossings with "a run of company sometimes on one side and sometimes on the other", especially as the other two large boats were fully employed carrying soldiers or sheep or cattle. If a horseman missed the hour boat and was presently joined by others, they might all decide to freight a small boat so that when the hour boat departed, it did so empty. Then there was the need to repair the boats which meant that at any one time some would be laid up. Another cause of discontinuity was the need to feed the crews. Incidentally the meals were provided on the North side. Finally certain classes of passenger required an immediate crossing: the mail, stage coaches and those joining passing steamers. Nevertheless despite the difficulties every effort was made to adhere to the hourly time table even if it meant carrying only a cart or a man and his horse, or even if it meant crossing empty to collect a couple of passengers on the other side.

Captain Scott made these observations in 1819. Four years later a Captain M'Konochie came to live at Northcliff. He was also ex navy and his house gave him a commanding view of the Ferry Passage. In 1828 Captain M'Konochie RN wrote his own "memorial" on the Ferry Passage which he passed to the trustees. He says that the mail for the whole of North Scotland arrived at Newhalls Inn at 7 30 pm and that the mail arrived at North Queensferry from the North at 5 30 am.   The boat was too small to embark the coach so bags and passengers had to be transferred.   There was a lot of waiting about on dark wet nights.   At the time of the great cattle fairs the ferry was so congested that the roads were "thronged for days together" and drovers were "forced to hire pastures about the Crossgates".   The four piers on each side were "kept sacred for ferry purposes alone" and because on the North side these piers occupied almost the whole sea frontage, the villagers were debarred from maritime trade.   This was keenly felt by the villagers.   He suggested two possible solutions - a road round the East of the Guildry promontory (Castle Hill) giving access to East Battery pier.   This would involve cutting through rock.   Alternatively the Town pier could be extended Northwards behind the Old and New Inns.   Captain M'Konochie was particularly scathing in his comments on the ferry.   He thought that the "Queen Margaret" was too expensive both to buy and to maintain.   Besides she frequently broke down.   There was little attention to punctuality: "not more than once in five or six times did the coach succeed in catching the steamer".   There was perhaps a touch of professional jealousy in his allegation that "the boats sailed as the Superintendent fancied".

At about the same time the trustees conducted their own investigation into the affairs of the Ferry. For this Thomas Telford was employed and made a special report. He felt that because the piers had been built for sailing vessels, a switch to entirely steam boats would be inadvisable.   In addition he found that the principal piers were not extended far enough into the water and were thus useless at very low tides, while East Battery pier had too abrupt a slope and was anyway too far to the East and therefore inconvenient. On the matter of boats he deferred to the wisdom of Captain Scott but agreed that another steam boat and a deep-waisted sailing vessel capable of carrying coaches would be advantageous.

Captain Scott's comments on the Ferry craft are instructive.   The sailing boats were rigged with a lug sail.   This was useful in backing the boats off the piers.   The square sail could be "reefed either by head or by foot".   This type of sail is shown in rough stone relief on the Waterloo Memorial at the bottom of the Brae. The type of rig meant that the ferry craft had neither bowsprit or boom.   Scott says that consequently there was less tackle to inconvenience the sailors when carrying bulky cargoes and when approaching the piers.   Furthermore there was ease in "backing or shivering in case of having too much way when approaching the piers .... the yard having much play, slung by its centre with a very slack wooden parrel, it comes freely down leaving no encumbrance aloft but the bare mast and tye block".   He ended his report by pointing out that the steamboat tows over two and sometimes three boats loaded with cattle and sheep besides herself carrying passengers, carriages, horses or carts. This allowed as many as 1000 head of cattle to be carried over per day at the time of the great fairs.

The trustees' report of 1828 gives us a fair idea of the finances of the ferry at this time.

Waterloo Memorial and the Brae

Rent payable by tacksmen	£1,720-00-0	
Allowance from Post Office	200-00-0	
	1,920-00-0	

Yearly average expense of maintaining steam-boat	£180-00-0	
Yearly expense of new flues and boilers supposing them to be required once in five years	170-00-0	
Yearly oil for light houses and other incidentals	80-00-0	
Yearly expense of sailing boats, supposing a new boat to be necessary once in ten years	50-00-0	
Yearly expense of repair on piers	94-00-0	
Rents and feu duty		
Town of Queensferry for use of harbour		
Scott Moncrieff	22-10-0	
Guildry of Dunfermline		
Interest on debts		
on £312-8-0 @ 5%	15-12-0	
on £15,375 bonds at 5%	768-15-0	
Salaries		
Mr Scott	120-00-0	
George Chisholm	54-12-0	
Clerks	60-00-0	£1,615-09-0
Annual Surplus		£304-11-0

Finally the trustees reached several conclusions. They decided to lengthen Signal House Pier (Town Pier, North Queensferry). This was finally completed in 1834. They decided that when one of the larger sailing boats came up for replacement, they would do so with a larger boat. They determined to buy a second steamboat when money would allow it; (if not a steamboat then at least a tug). They also decided not to experiment with towing flat lighters across. Finally they concluded that "interference of other traffic other than that which belongs to a ferry, on piers used by a ferry is inconsistent with its perfectness". In this they appear to have had their eyes on South Queensferry. We have seen from Captain M'Konochie's memorial that they had already beaten the North Queensferry residents into submission by monopolising the sea front. South Queensferry was larger however and a tougher nut to crack. For this an Act of Parliament was necessary. The result of this final proposal was the Water Passage Bill of 1830, by which the ferry trustees claimed jurisdiction over the harbour and free port of South Queensferry. South Queensferry residents were adamant in their opposition to the Bill and organised a series of protest meetings, one of which was held at North Queensferry.

The trustees explained that the new Bill was by no means intended to infringe upon any of the vested rights of the Royal Burgh of Queensferry. This form of double talk failed to impress the local residents. Moreover they appear to have won their case, for following the passing of the Act the ferry ceased to use South Queensferry harbour, from then on using only Long Craig, the Hawes, and Port Edgar piers on the South side. By the Water Passage Act the ferry was vested in new trustees; new tariffs were introduced and the limits of the ferry were defined.

Hey days of coaching

The era after the Napoleonic War and before the coming of the train was the hey-day of coaching. North Queensferry with its thirteen places "where spirit may be bought in small quantities and drunk upon the premises" was well-placed to benefit from the passing traffic. The principal inns were the Old and New Inns. The former no longer exists. It stood on the east side of the road at the head of Signal House Pier and had stables behind it. It was also known as Mrs Malcolm's Inn. The latter still stands and is known today as the Albert Hotel. It was known then as Mitchell's Inn and was built on a site formerly occupied by the Hope Tavern. It seems to have been designed specifically to cater for the coaching trade and therefore dates from the first half of the 19th century. Its stables were on the opposite side of the road, down by the water. The remains of these still exist. This inn appears to have been the more important of the two. In the early coaching period the steepness of the Brae was a source of inconvenience. Before the improvements to the Great North Road the coach ran over the old road to Inverkeithing, ie up the Brae with its tortuous turns and its one in five gradient. In the opposite direction passengers got out of the coach at the top of the hill and descended on foot to the passage boat.

Several coaches passed through the village. One of the best known was the Defiance, run by a Captain Barclay on the route between Edinburgh and Aberdeen. He was coachman both on the inaugural run in 1829 and the coach's final journey in 1849. He was otherwise known as the "celebrated pedestrian" because he had once won a 1,000 guinea bet that he could walk 1,000 miles in 1,000 hours. There was nothing pedestrian about his coach service however. It had such a record for time keeping that people set their watches and clocks by "Defiance time". The first ten miles of the journey, from Princes Street to South Queensferry were covered in a miraculous 50 minutes. The whole route was timed to the last minute. Barclay bragged "She'll be in Aberdeen by 7.10 if naethin' happens tae Aberdeen".

Another well-known coach commenced in 1825 on the route between Edinburgh and Dunfermline. This was a yellow coach run by Croalls. Its driver wore a red coat with yellow bands and a lum hat with red bands. This pretty sight could be seen leaving Princes Street at 7.15 am every day, and returning every afternoon. At first it had only two horses and a contemporary refers to it disparagingly as the Queensferry "noddy". Later it was replaced with a four-in-hand coach running three times a day. The coach appears to have been called "The Antiquary" after Scott's antiquary who caught a coach at South Queensferry.

which he refers to as the "Hawes Fly". This coach carried the mail on some journeys and continued on this route until it was forced out of existence by the railway in 1878. Brock lists the drivers of this coach in the 1850's and 1860's as Peter Hume, William Hunter, William Robertson, George Aitken and Adam Watt. The hostler at North Queensferry was called Cunningham, which was pronounced "Kinnicum". He was also known as "Garvie Molly". On the South side Will Ewing was the hostler. When a traveller disappointed him by not giving him a tip, he observed "If ye lose yer purse Sir, remember ye hadna it oot here".

Other coaches using the ferry were the Royal Mail to Aberdeen and the Saxe Coburg to Perth. Some of the following coaches may also have crossed here: The Kingdom of Fife, The Royal Union, The Tally Ho and The Flying Machine. All these were bound for Dundee. The latter had six horses. Its adverts boasted that it ran "every Tuesday God willing and every Wednesday whether or no".

The ferry was indeed a busy place. In 1836 the Reverend Andrew Robertson described the village as follows: "a flourishing village inhabited by the boatmen principally and much resorted to in summer as sea-bathing quarters. The piers are unrivalled and there is an elegant and commodious inn lately built". In the first part of the 19th century the following list of ferry users gives a good idea of how busy the village would have been:

40	Hearses
145	Coaches
465	Chaises
16	Curricles
770	Gigs
1,580	Carriage Horses
4,110	Carts
4,310	Carts and horses
5,860	Saddle horses
31	Mules and asses
16,000	Black cattle
30	Calves and hogs
23,300	Sheep
3,600	Lambs
2,340	Dogs
4,500	Barrel bulk of goods and luggage
77,500	Passengers
3,500	Highland shearers

In addition mails, guards, military baggage carts, troops and government stores.

We get a more personal view of the ferry and of its place in the scheme of things by the account of a young builder in the North. He decided to "first fit" his people in Edinburgh at Hogmanay 1830. He set out before dawn arriving at North Queensferry at night fall "where to my great disappointment there were no boats going on account of the stormy night. My only chance now was to wait for the Defiance coach (Edinburgh - Aberdeen) .... She came up about two o'clock being nearly three hours after her time and in

about half an hour the passengers were called to the coach boat. It was a small pinnace. The coach being full it was given out that none save coach passengers were to be allowed to get across". He managed to get across by a stratagem but was "nearly nicked". He continues: "We made a quick run across and our boat grounded below the Hawes but we got her afloat again and made the pier where with a light heart I jumped on shore on my own side of the Forth". While the others stopped at The Hawes Inn to drink in the New Year, he took to the road on a fine frosty moonlit night. The coach passed him at the fourth milestone but he met no one else until he came to Mutton Hole (Davidsons Mains). He ends: "As I passed along Heriot Row I heard ... the clock strike three o'clock".

Meanwhile the ferry had its share of problems. The traffic was growing, but it could so easily be tempted away. The combination of river steamers plying up and down the river and ferry crossings at other points gave rise to fierce competition. With its aging steamship, piers built for sailing vessels and lack of money available for investment, the trustees did what they could. Signal House Pier was extended into deeper water, taking its final shape in 1834. A few years later a wooden jetty was added to enable the passing steamers to call, so that before the middle of the century Stirling and Alloa steamers were able to land passengers here. The new wooden extension however was not a success and later it was demolished. Following this David McRitchie, known as "Priest Davie", provided a "floorying" service taking passengers on and off the passing steamers in his lug sail yawl. In 1838 the trustees made a bid to retrieve the situation. They themselves put together enough money to purchase the "William Adam" a steam vessel twice as powerful as the "Queen Margaret" which now went out of use. The new vessel cost £2,800 and consumed 3 tons of coal per day. Provost James Morison of South Queensferry described her as follows "She had no upper deck amidships in order to allow room or headway for the upper part of her piston gear of the old fashioned vertical engine, and across this space ran the narrow bridge from which the captain gave his orders direct to the engineer". The "William Adam" left the South side every hour and the North side every half hour between sunrise and sunset. Sailing vessels were less needed now and were reduced to 2 boats and 2 pinnaces. The "William Adam" enabled a better time table to be kept: "Travellers know the very minute when they can procure a passage and by well regulated signals when on the water can secure the presence of a carriage awaiting them on their arrival at the pier where civil porters and hostlers connected with the establishments on shore consult the comfort and convenience of passengers who may calculate on crossing in 10 or 12 minutes". These mannerly and solicitous porters are a far cry from the unruly bunch who abused the 17th century passenger. The ferry crossing, besides being more genteel, was now quicker, more regular and much safer - all benefits of the great spirit of progress which rolled the 19th century forward. But even efficient operators are unable to prevent all mishaps. A few months after the new vessel started on the passage the Saxe Coburg coach was being wheeled down the quay at Newhalls to transfer passengers to the ferry when it lurched and fell into the water.

South Queensferry Harbour

The coach landed on its side so that two passengers were able to put their heads through the windows until rescued; two others, a girl and an elderly woman servant were drowned. The Scotsman commented that "the melancholy result is entirely attributable to the dangerous practice recently introduced of loading the coach on the quay instead of at the inn as formerly and at the same time leaving the horses' heads unattended".

Captain Scott retires : Queensferry in decline

The next year Captain James Scott, Superintendent of the Ferry Passage for almost 30 years and now aged 72, decided to retire. Upon the introduction of the "William Adam" he had been presented with a silver service. Now on his retirement he refused a £50 pension from the trustees on the grounds of its cost to the ferry passage. However, the Sailors' Society of which he was president made him a presentation. Fortunately he had several years of retirement to enjoy these gifts. He died at the age of 83 in 1850. The memorial in Inverkeithing Churchyard reads:

"Battles had seen and Sailed in various Climes
Thousands of Beings saw in latter Times
Ferried in safety back and fore to Fife
With Christian Hope he crossed the Sea of Life"

Behind the epitaph lies a long and eventful life. He started out as a clerk at Fordell colliery but enlisted for the navy. He served under Admiral Duncan and was present at the mutiny of the Nore and at the battle of Camperdown, aboard the 64 gun, Belliqueux. He was also under Nelson at the Battle of the Baltic. At some stage he was also a press gang leader. When he came to North Queensferry the trustees bought Seabank Cottage for him "giving him a complete view of the passage". The move was not popular locally and he was warned that Seabank was haunted, to which he replied to the effect that he had a loaded gun, ready for the ghost whenever it liked to come. He was desribed in the 1830's as "pretty well advanced in life and hardly straight in his figure" yet "active in his habits, springy in his movements and buoyant in his manners". He is said to have broken one or both legs. Many people thought that this would have been the end of him but he got back on his feet. "Most of his dress was in the pink of almost youthful fashion with a broad brimmed beaver hat that inclined a little towards his shoulders and from it hung a queue or pigtail". On one occasion he went to make peace between a drunken man and his wife. The man roared at him and ran for his gun, but the resourceful Captain retreated, zig-zagging up the close to avoid being hit. It is also said that the Countess of Elgin would never cross the ferry without him, (although this may tell us more about the Countess than the Captain).

A lot of Captain Scott's working life would have been spent at the Signal House, (the hexagonal building to which an extension has been added, at the extreme South of the village overlooking the piers). This was built around 1810 and was used as an administrative centre for the ferry. Below, it had a waiting room for the use of travellers about to cross the ferry. Above, there was a room with an eight-sided table at which the trustees sat to conduct formal business. It became known as Mount Hooly because it took so long to build. Hooly is an archaic word meaning slowly and cannily, as in "Hooly and fairly gangs far in a day". In 1824 the body of a Captain Gurley rested here under a Union Jack, after a duel between him and a Mr Westall. The dispute had started in "The Bull" in Edinburgh and concerned a bet at the Doncaster races. The two men were unable to settle their dispute and so appointed seconds. They and their seconds crossed to North Queensferry and climbed to near the top of the Ferryhills. (The exact spot is marked by a large upright stone and lies due East of the present water house). The weapons chosen were pistols. Captain Gurley was shot dead. Later his wife came to claim the body which was buried in Inverkeithing Churchyard (incidentally in a mort-cloth which the North Queensferry Sailors' Society hired out for 4 shillings).

Captain Scott's assistant at Mount Hooly was one Wullie Greig. We learn from Brock that he courted Scott's successive maids, but although the Captain often warned "now the knot must be tied", Greig never married. Brock continues "Wullie had one unfailing greeting for everybody he met winter and summer, namely "Its awfy cauld the day". When he was on night duty at Mount Hooly, on the look-out for blazes and signals, the ferry boys used to go to the window and listen to him saying his prayers. These, strangely enough, were to the effect that the Lord would send him "oceans of whisky and mountains of cheese". The boys would then knock on his window and scamper off with the old man after them. Having chased them round the village he would return to his prayer which was the same every night. Willie had two tones of voice, one a shrill squealing treble, the other a deep basso profoundo. Captain Scott used often to chaff and sometimes to chide Willie who would take offence for the time being, and would retire to some corner he had in the Signal House and say his prayers in his two voices. He prayed so that Captain Scott could hear him "O Lord hae mercy on me but hae nae mercy on that man up the stair for he has nae mercy on me".

Captain Scott's period as ferry Superintendent was one of dramatic change. He came at a time when the ferry was in urgent need of modernisation. He witnessed the changes which brought its sailing boats to a peak of efficiency, only to find that the advent of steam made those changes obsolete within a few years of their completion. He himself designed the first steamship on the passage in order to win back the custom which had been lost to the steam vessels of the Broad Ferry. When the "Queen Margaret" showed signs of obsolescence he advised on its replacement with the "William Adam". Latterly he saw the ferry win back its

position of pre-eminence as a Forth crossing point. He also saw the village itself grow in importance and prosperity, (despite the final severing of the villagers' grip on working the ferry and the virtual monopoly that the trustees established over the use of the water-front). Very soon after his retirement however, the Edinburgh Leith and Granton Railway opened offering rapid access via Burntisland to the North. Once more, the village and its ferry faced economic decline.

It seems fitting that in the final days of coaching prosperity Queen Victoria and Prince Albert should have visited the village. In their honour the pier was carpeted with red cloth and triumphal arches were erected in the Main Street. For the crossing Mr Mason, the Superintendent, took the helm while the skipper Charles Roxburgh, attended to other duties. On the Northern shore the Queen paused to survey the scene and asked the retired Superintendent, Captain Scott to point out one of the islands. He is reported to have replied "Its straucht fornent your Majesty", which may not have clarified the subject but must have added a strong dash of local colour to the royal visit.

Mount Hooly and Signal House Pier, looking North.

CHAPTER VI

Bridging the Forth

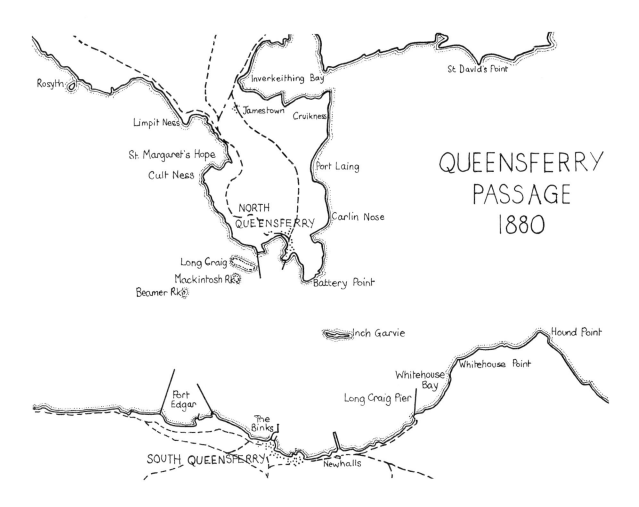

QUEENSFERRY PASSAGE 1880

The Edinburgh-Leith-Granton railway opened in 1846. The next year a railway was opened on the North side running North from Burntisland to Cupar and Lindores. In 1848 these two branches were extended to Ferryport-on-Craig (on the Tay estuary opposite Dundee) and to Perth respectively. Thus the direct route North from Edinburgh now ran via Burntisland. The engineer of the Edinburgh Perth and Dundee railway was Thomas Bouch. He now devised a floating railway so that railway wagons could be run directly onto the Burntisland ferries without transhipment of their cargoes. The scheme had been intended to apply to both goods and passenger trains but in fact it was used only for the former. Even so, the Broad Ferry now became the most popular Forth crossing point. Passengers spent longer on the boat than they would have done at Queensferry, but their total

journey time was now reduced because of the superiority of rail over the stage coach. On the boat there was sometimes entertainment from a blind harmonium player and a fiddler. One of their pieces was entitled "Auld Man's Mare" and went like this:

> "The auld man's mares deid
> The puir man's mares deid
> The auld man's mares deid
> A mile aboon Dundee
>
> She was cut luggit, painch lippit
> Steel waimit, staincher fittit
> Chanler chaftit, lang neckit
> And yet the brute did dee"

The Charlestown crossing was never crucially important. It nevertheless provided a well-

used service.   Something over 20,000 passengers
a year crossed at this point in the period
1838-43.   Its popularity increased however with
the building of a pier at which the steamers could
touch (so that passengers no longer had to be
rowed out to catch the Ferry), and increased even
further in 1852 when steam was introduced on the
railway line between Charlestown and Dunfermline.

In the face of competition of this sort the
people of Queensferry and the ferry trustees
could do little but wait.   Inevitably, in due
course the powerful railway companies would
reconsider the many attractions of the

RAILWAY LINKS
1852

Queensferry strait.   The decline of Queensferry
was immediate and profound.   What had been a
bustling ferry, with a hundred or more posting
horses became something of a ghost town.
Mitchell's Inn, later renamed The Albert, which
had been built for the coaching trade, fell into
disuse and was soon to be split up into flats,
one of which was later used for prayer meetings.

Queensferry fights back

The railway finally reached North Queensferry in
1877, when a solid stone slipway was built to
give access between the station and the ferry
boats.   The station was built at the head of the
pier, the latter being called Railway Pier then,
and Marina Pier now signifying its recent change
of use.   The line ran from Inverkeithing along
the West side of the Queensferry peninsular
and was carried via a tunnel under the hillside,
and a cutting on the site of present day Inchcolm
Drive to its terminus.   The link between
Dunfermline and North Queensferry had been long-
planned.   Luckily an earlier scheme proposed
by the Edinburgh and Glasgow Railway in 1862 was
turned down.   It would have had two termini
one at Marina Pier;   the other at Signal House
Pier.   Thus a line would have run right across
West Bay to meet the ferry boats in the middle of
the village.   On the rejection of this scheme
the church bells were rung for an hour in
celebration in Inverkeithing and Dunfermline.   An
Act of Parliament the following year enabled
the Edinburgh Perth and Dundee Railway to acquire
the ferry from the trustees, thus giving the
railway a monopoly of carrying passengers over
the water.   The cost of the deal was £4,500 plus
£200 legal expenses, a price which is eloquent of
the decline of the Queensferry crossing in the mid
19th century.   Fifty years previously almost double
this had been paid to purchase the ferry from its
private owners, and immediately following this
well over £30,000 had been spent on improvements.
The railway company continued the practise of
leasing the ferry to tacksmen.   The idea behind
the purchase was that the Edinburgh and Glasgow
Railway would build a line linking Ratho and
South Queensferry.   The North British Railway
which commanded the important East Coast route

from England to Edinburgh would acquire running
rights over this track.   At the same time the
Edinburgh Perth and Dundee would establish a link
to the North from North Queensferry.   In the event,
both the smaller companies were taken over by the
North British, which then became owner of the
ferry passage.   In 1866 the link on the Southern
shore reached Dalmeny (then known as New Halls),
passengers having to climb from the water side
up to the station above the Hawes Inn to catch
the trains.   Six years later, work started on
the line between Dunfermline and North Queensferry.
This took five years to complete.   Following its
opening the line on the Southern shore was
extended to Port Edgar thus giving the maximum
convenience to passengers short of actually
building a bridge.   From this time to the
opening of the Forth Railway Bridge (1890) the
ferries plied principally between Port Edgar on
the South (protected by a 1,300 foot breakwater)
and Railway pier on the North.   They also called
at New Halls on the South, tides permitting, and
at Signal House Pier on the North.

When the railway company acquired the ferry it
also acquired the obsolescent ferry boat "William
Adam".   This 49 ton iron-hulled vessel was now
transferred to Burntisland for less onerous
duties and its place taken by "Nymph".   The latter
had been built in 1851 and was acquired by the
NBR from owners in Liverpool.   She was heavier
and more powerful than her predecessor but failed
to give a satisfactory service, having inadequate
power to combat all states of the local tides.
Brodie, whose "Steamers of the Forth" provides
an authoritative source of information, observes
that "when the flood passes Queensferry, it
develops whirls towards the shores and for the
first hour while the tide is flowing in mid-stream
it is still ebbing at the sides .... The ebb is
very fast and rips through the windings (above
Alloa) at twelve to fourteen knots, but reduces to
eight by the time it reaches Queensferry .... even
so, calls between Alloa and Queensferry were difficult
and if mooring ropes were not caught first throw,

it was a struggle to get the ship back to the pier".
In illustrating the difficulties of the tide at
Queensferry, Brodie mentions that "Until 1964 when
the ferry service ceased, all vessels ran with
three black balls permanently fixed to their
signal lanyard signifying "Keep clear; I am
out of control".

Ferry boats adrift

On New Years Day 1877 "Nymph" broke loose from her
moorings and would have been wrecked. Fortunately
five fishermen boarded her and were able to bring
the vessel to safety. Each received 10/- as a
reward. By this time the railway company had
decided that a more effective vessel would be needed
in view of the increased traffic expected from
railway passengers. They ordered a new vessel from
J Key and Sons of Kinghorn and named her "John
Beaumont" after one of the railway company directors.
The new ferry was heavier and more powerful than
"Nymph" and had a shallow draught and square ends,
suited to ferry working. She was driven by
screw propulsion but disappointingly was capable of
only 7 knots. This gave insufficient power to
handle well in all states of wind and tide. The
directors realising this cancelled the sale of "Nymph"
with what appears to have been admirable timing for
in December 1878 "John Beaumont" went out of control,
struck the railway pier and sank. The event
was commemorated by a villager in the following
terms:

Oh! what will the directors think
Their boat sae braw sae bonny
Is lying low among the slink (1)
The Johnny! Oh! The Johnny!

Thus sadly mourned the rescued tars
About their sunken steamer
Says Sandy 'Ye may thank yer stars
She didna sink off Beamer (2)

When Skipper Jack had heard the news
Oot spak that ancient gaffer
The NBR noo sairly rues
The day they put me aff her (3)

Some men hae focht in foreign climes
And never got a scar yet
I've crossed the Forth ten thousand times
And never lost a spar yet

Directors of the NBR
Ye ne'er should fash to lift her
Ye've mony better boats by far
The Willie e'en was swifter (4)

Ye'll find that paddles beat the screw
Although ye've sair misca'd them
Nor could ye wish a smarter crew
Than sailed the Willie Adam

But when the Northern shore was near
Away she rushed careerin'
And dowly headed past the pier
Regardless o' the steerin '

In vain in vain was a' oor wark
She up the tide gaed dartin'
Then lumbrin' roun' like Noah's Ark
Gaed sideways like a partan (5)

Then some ran fore and some ran aft
Ilk cried what he thocht proper
The engineer was clean dang daft
Wi' Ease Her! Back Her! Stop her!

Our ancient tars were sairly miss'd
They were sae smart and handy
Since Jamie's frae the pier dismiss'd
There's nane left noo but Sandy

At last wi' mony a heavy roll
She on the pier gaed jarrin'
Wi sic a dunt she ca'd a hole
Clean through her starboard starn

A gallant effort then was made
To run her up and beach her
And get her in a saft place laid
Where tempests ne'er could reach her

But oh! The flood comes in apace
And soon the Johnny founders
To find a quiet resting place
Far down among the flounders

Attributed to Robert Robertson
of Dean Cottage

The John Beaumont

(1) Slink: mud
(2) Beamer: rock to the West of present
         road bridge
(3) Jockie Anderson had been skipper of
     the "William Adam" and "Nymph" and

was for a time skipper of the "John
Beaumont"
(4) The "William Adam"
(5) Partan: crab

The "John Beaumont" was repaired and converted to a paddle steamer. In 1879 "Thane of Fife", which had been used on the Tay Ferry, was transferred to Queensferry and became the principal ferry boat. "John Beaumont" was used as back up when "Thane of Fife" was being over-hauled, and with her new paddles, proved a useful and reliable vessel. She was sold by the NBR in 1894 and was finally to work in Istanbul under the name "Gul Bahtche".

Tunnel or bridge?

Ferries were an expensive and inconvenient means of crossing the Forth. It was inevitable that once time and technology were right, a bridge would provide a neater and more permanent solution. The earliest suggestion however was for a tunnel. At the very time the Queensferry and Perth Turnpike Road Trustees were considering what to do about the inadequacies of the Queensferry Passage, another group of gentlemen in Edinburgh were proposing a scheme for avoiding the passage altogether. The proponents were Messrs John Grieve, James Taylor and William Vazie, who encouraged by submarine tunnels elsewhere (notably the coal workings at nearby Borrowstonness) planned a tunnel running between Rosyth and South Queensferry. They proposed two alternatives: two passages each 15 feet high and 12 feet wide with a raised pedestrian way in each, or a single tunnel 24 feet wide with a central raised pedestrian way. Their prospectus issued by "a number of noblemen and gentlemen of the first respectability and scientific character" invited subscriptions for shares at £100 each. The Scots Magazine called it a "work in the highest degree curious and important" but the investing public thought otherwise and the project was dropped.

In 1818 James Anderson Civil Engineer of Edinburgh revived interest in the Queensferry crossing with his "Design for a chain bridge thrown over the Firth of Forth at Queensferry". This time the chosen site was that of the present railway bridge where "the appearance and situation are altogether so favourable and so inviting for some work of art .... that a bridge of some description ought to be attempted". Anderson proposed three possible versions. All used Inch Garvie as a stepping stone. The cheapest at £144,000 had 3 spans and 90 foot headroom for ships at high water; the most expensive at £170,000 had 4 spans and 110 foot headroom. The question of headroom was of interest to local commercial interests so Anderson made a special visit to Leith to measure the height of a 400 ton vessel. He found that it would need 108 feet of headroom, leaving 2 feet clearance on the most expensive design. The bridge was to be 34 feet broad with two pathways each 4 feet wide. A contemporary illustration shows a disproportionately large horse and cart crossing the bridge. The bridge would be built of iron and oak, the former being heated and dipped in linseed oil to halt corrosion. It would take an estimated four years to build. Again, the project failed to gain support. Seventy years later a bridge engineer remarked that the bridge of chains "was so light a structure that it would heardly have been visible on a dull day and after a heavy gale it would no longer be seen on a clear day either".

Plans for a permanent crossing at Queensferry were now dropped for several decades. Then in 1851 Mr Thomas Bouch, an engineer of rising eminence, proposed a system of floating pontoons to carry railway carriages across. He had pioneered a similar scheme on the Burntisland-Granton crossing but this had never carried passenger trains. Consequently his plans for Queensferry found little support. Several years later however, the same engineer proposed a bridge linking Charlestown with Blackness. Here the water was shallower than at Queensferry and there would be less danger to shipping. The bridge would be over two miles long and be sited in up to 60 feet of water, giving the North British Railway access from Edinburgh to Aberdeen and the North. The proposal was for a lattice girder construction costing £500,000 to carry a single line track on 61 piers. The track would be more than 100 feet above the water, and in the centre would cross 4 spans each 500 feet long. In 1864/5 bore holes were sunk to establish the feasibility of building piers. They went down 166-231 feet without clearing the silt or striking bed-rock. Besides suffering from physical difficulties, the proposals were opposed by other railway companies and by the Alloa Harbour and Clyde Navigation Trusts. In view of Bouch's subsequent connection with the ill-fated Tay Railway Bridge, the hearings concerning this proposal contain a fascinating series of exchanges.

Counsel for the opponents suggested that wind pressure on the bridge might cause the base columns to sink. Bouch replied:

> "Certainly not. I have built bridges of similar kind and find nothing of the sort". "Was that in a narrow glen and upon dry land?" "Yes, it was upon dry land but it was in Westmoreland which is subject to great gales." "Supposing it were to happen that one of these columns should get loose .... and that it would sink a little lower, what would be the effect on the structure?" "You may as well ask me to assume that it will come down ..."

Bouch won the day and an Act was passed allowing

the North British to erect the bridge. Before
embarking on full scale construction however
the company decided to test its feasibility by
erecting one pier. An enormous raft was
launched at Burntisland and towed into position.
Work began on the pier which was to be a brick-
work shell containing 10,000 tons of iron.
But on Friday 3rd August 1866 a party of
directors who apparently had come to inspect
progress ordered work to cease, the reason
being that the North British Railway was
virtually bankrupt. The workment were sacked
and the project abandoned. The cost had been
£34,390.

Bouch's third scheme for crossing the Forth was
his last and like the others, abortive. The
Forth Bridge Company had been formed in 1873
and an Act of the same year gave permission for
a bridge at Queensferry. It was to be a double
suspension bridge with two spans each 1,600 feet
long. Two central towers on Inch Garvie,
550 feet high, would provide headroom of 150 feet
at high tide and would carry twin railway
tracks 100 feet apart. A consortium of railway
companies agreed to subscribe the capital.
The contract was let to Messrs William Arrol
who erected workshops at South Queensferry.
Work had already started on siting the piers
on Inch Garvie, and the foundation stone had
been laid, when news broke that Bouch's Tay
Bridge had collapsed.

The story of this spectacular tragedy has been
told by John Prebble. It is a tangent to our
narrative. Briefly, this bridge was constructed
between 1871 and 1877 under the supervision of
Sir Thomas Bouch. Its design was similar to
the proposed bridge linking Charlestown and
Blackness, consisting of 85 spans, on cast
iron piers sited in fairly shallow water. On
the last Sunday of 1879 on a night of gale
force winds, 1,000 yards of the bridge collapsed
while a train was upon it. All 75 travellers
were killed. Subsequently a Court of Enquiry
found that the bridge "was badly designed, badly
constructed and badly maintained and its
downfall was due to inherent defects in the
structure which must sooner or later have
brought it down. For these defects both in
design construction and maintenance Sir Thomas
Bouch is in our opinion mainly to blame". Five
months later Bouch died at the age of 58, and
so did his plans for a Forth bridge.

The railway bridge

The collapse of the Tay Bridge was a setback to the
Victorians' faith in irresistible progress, and
particularly in their confidence in civil
engineers. It is therefore remarkable that
only three years separate this event from the
start of work on a new Forth Railway Bridge of
revolutionary design. An important cause of
the collapse had been intense lateral wind
pressure which had not been properly anticipated
or allowed for in the design. The engineers
of the new Forth Bridge, Messrs John Fowler and
Benjamin Baker, were aware of this. Their
bridge was to be broader at the base than at
the top in the form of a straddle, and in addition
was to be braced to withstand lateral wind
pressure of up to 56 pounds per square foot.
This was well in excess of readings taken on
Inch Garvie during the course of construction
which were mostly in the range of 18 - 30
pounds per square feet. Many of the techniques
used to build the bridge were previously unknown
and it fell to the engineers to solve problems
from first principles. For instance the
apparatus used to measure wind pressure was
designed by them, especially for the purpose.

The bridge was constructed on the cantilever
principle; that is to say each half-span
formed a bracket. Each tower, of which there
were three, carried a half span on either side,
so that the method of construction was to build
the towers first and then from either side
of these to build the brackets (at equal rates
to avoid toppling the towers). Finally the
brackets extending from the towers had to be
joined in the middle at their furthest
points from the towers. The whole then
formed a solid and well-balanced structure, the
railway being carried along on a continuous
girder. The principle was demonstrated by
Fowler and Baker with the help of two of their
workmen and a junior engineer Kaichi Watanabe
from Japan. They are shown in a contemporary
photo from which the sketch on this page has
been taken. With Mr Watanabe on the "bridge"
the arms of the men are brought into tension and
the men's bodies and the chairs and rods come
into compression. Generally on the railway
bridge itself the arms of the men are
represented by lattice girders and the other
parts by hollow circular steel tubes. Here

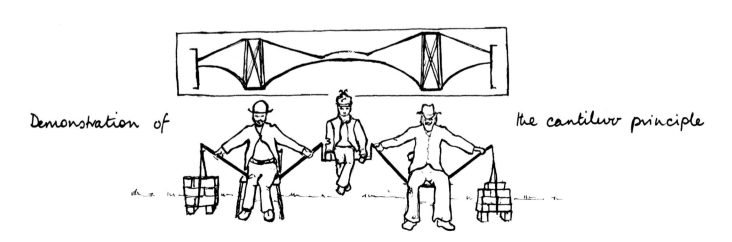

Demonstration of   the cantilever principle

again, it was left to the engineers to discover which cross-section of hollow steel tube would be strongest under the conditions given. They experimented and chose the circular section.

The Act of Parliament for building the bridge was obtained in 1883; the bridge was opened in 1890. The intervening years divide into two equal periods:

1882 - 1886   Construction of the piers on which the bridge rests

1886 - 1890   Erection of the super-structure of the bridge itself

The bridge rests on three main foundations; one at North Queensferry; one on Inch Garvie and the other out from South Queensferry. Each foundation is composed of four separate round columns of stone. Construction of the North Queensferry foundation was reasonably easy because it is situated between the high and low water mark (today, the visible parts are all on dry land and can be inspected at close quarters). On Inch Garvie however two of the stone columns are situated in deep water, and on the South Queensferry side all four columns are in deep water. All these deep water piers were constructed with the use of caissons. These were huge wrought iron barrels, each weighing as much as 500 tons and measuring 70 foot in diameter and 50-60 feet in height. They were constructed on shore, floated out from South Queensferry and sunk in the exact position of each pier. Once in position the lower edge was cut into the bedrock. Then the air pressure inside the caisson was increased to prevent seepage of water. The result was a watertight space inside the caisson in which construction of the piers could take place. The space was 7 foot high and enabled workmen to sink the caissons to the required depth and then to build strong masonry piers. The air pressure inside was as high as 35 lbs per square inch. On one occasion a visitor to the works took a glass flask of spirits with him which he drank during the visit. On returning to the normal atmosphere the empty flask exploded: the pressure inside was too great for the strength of the glass.

Construction of the foundations of the bridge was a laborious but essential process. The piers on Inch Garvie were completed by March 1885. One pier at South Queensferry however caused considerable delay. The caisson was sunk but filled with water and got stuck in the wrong position. It took three months to float it up by pumping the water out, but then the iron of the empty caisson buckled under the pressure of the water outside. Finally they decided to make a watertight timber "skin" for the caisson. The work was slow because the timber had to be fitted by divers. Finally however the caisson was correctly sited and this last pier was completed in March 1886.

The first phase in building the superstructure was the erection of three main towers. Each tower was composed of four steel tubes, one for each of the four stone piers. The tubes which are 12 feet in diameter slope inwards. Thus at their base they are 120 feet apart and at their summit (360 feet above high-water)

they are only 33 feet apart. With the towers complete it was necessary to build outwards on the side of each tower at the same rate so that each tower remained in equilibrium. Thus huge steel brackets were formed overhanging the water. Finally the overhanging ends were joined by extending a continuous girder between them. This method allowed the bridge itself to be the scaffolding for its own construction, and was necessary because no free standing scaffolding could be erected over the water. During construction the bridge bristled with cranes and platforms. The steel which was used, was shaped and drilled at South Queensferry. It was then shipped out and hoisted into position. Finally the workmen riveted it using enormous hydraulic rams designed by William Arrol, the principal of Messrs Tancred Arrol and Co Ltd who were contractors for the project.

The workmen

Most of the activity occurred on the South side where sheds were constructed for drilling, planing and bending the steel which arrived by train from Glasgow and South Wales. A jetty was constructed below the Hawes Inn so that materials could be shipped out conveniently. On the North side, the East battery slipway was used for a similar purpose. Amongst the newcomers to North Queensferry were a concrete mixer, stone crusher and cement shed in the vicinity of St James Bay, and workmen's accommodation to the West of Signal House Pier and in the centre of the village. Accommodation was a problem. During construction of the superstructure large numbers of workmen were employed on the bridge, varying with the work and the seasons:

1887	(Spring)	3,200
	(Autumn)	4,100
1888 - 1889	(Winter)	2,900
1890		1,000

The maximum number at any one time was in the region of 4,600. Obviously insufficient accommodation was available in South and North Queensferry. Some took up residence a little further afield. Many others came in by special train from Edinburgh (weekly ticket 2/-) and Dunfermline (weekly ticket 1/-). Several hundred workmen came from Leith, rising at 4.00 am in order to be at work at 6.00 am and returning home by 7.00 pm. It was not always possible to locate men on the side most convenient for their homes. As a result a fleet of vessels was necessary to carry them to and from their places of work.

At work there were large shelters, canteens and dining rooms, either on the deck of the bridge or up in the towers or on the cantilevers. For the most part the workmen were hard-working resourceful and dependable. Sir Benjamin Baker described the bridge as "essentially a workmen's bridge", the success of which was due to their "individual and collective pluck and ingenuity, as much as to the labours of engineers and contractors". One workman summed it all up thus "the men were aye brave and cheery and the muckle brig went up wi' a song".

This was not of course the whole story. Working at varying heights one above the other and with heavy tools and materials, accidents were inevitable. The stagings from which the workmen worked were littered with tools and equipment so that "hammers and drifts and chisels and pieces of wood .... in a moment were over the side and tumbled down upon maybe three or four other tiers of staging where men were engaged upon their work". Special gangs were employed to keep the stagings clear but accidents still occurred. On one occasion Sir Benjamin Baker saw a hole 1 inch in diameter made through a 4 inch thick timber by a spanner which had dropped 300 feet. On another a dropped spanner entered a man's waistcoat and came out at his ankle tearing open his clothes but doing him no injury. The conditions of their work and their growing familiarity with it made some workmen unnecessarily careless. Boys were seen "jumping from plank to plank in the upper works as if the distance below them was of no consideration whatsoever" and there was amongst some an "utter indifference or carelessness with regard to danger of causing injuries or death to one another. Not that in cases of sudden accident men would have hesitated to risk limb or life for the sake of helping". Some survived their accident. Below each cantilever was a rowing boat manned by two expert watermen. These saved 8 lives and collected 8,000 or so pieces of

In 1883 a Sick and Accident Club was formed. Membership was compulsory and the subscription was one hour's pay per week limited to a maximum of 8d per week. The club dispensed medical advice, medicines and bandages. Allowances were granted for unemployment and for those not fit to work (9/- - 12/- per week to cover food). Grants were also made to widows and towards funeral expenses. Besides contributing £200 annually to the club the contractors also in the case of accident paid the wages of the injured man until he "was able to return to work or unless an action was raised against the contractors".

The opening

The new bridge was opened on 4th March 1890 by the Prince of Wales. He marked the occasion by fixing a golden commemorative rivet. A special programme was printed and illustrated with a picture of Edinburgh castle and of a locomotive named "Progress". The destination board reads "through carriage Aberdeen to New York via Tay Bridge, Forth Bridge, Channel Tunnel and Alaska" and in the bottom corner it says "of dazzling great adventures, this the foremost". It was blowing a gale during the opening ceremony and

STAGES IN THE CONSTRUCTION OF THE FORTH RAIL BRIDGE

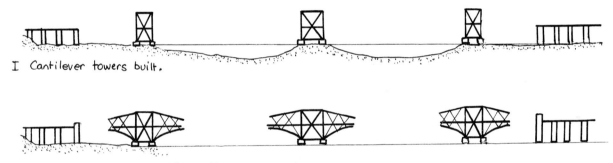

I Cantilever towers built.

II Balanced construction of cantilevers proceeds.

III Cantilevers extended to form continuous girder.

clothing which the wind had blown into the water. Thus the man who trusted himself to grasping a rope at 120 feet and then grew numb and relaxed his hold, fell into the sea and was recovered. Another who went up by hoist without fixing the rail, was less lucky. He fell 180 feet to his death carrying away a dozen rungs of a ladder with which he came into contact during his fall. In all there were 57 deaths and 518 "minor" accidents during construction.

the Prince's top hat was reputedly blown off. Anyway the formalities were cut short and the party repaired to a banqueting hall at South Queensferry. There it was announced that Fowler, Baker and Arrol had all been knighted. In his reply to the Prince of Wales, Sir John Fowler observed "the workmen have been chiefly Scottish. They are famous throughout the world for their work as masons especially in granite .... With Scottish granite and English cement we have durability and union of parts for at least a thousand years." The only threats to the steel would be oxidisation and vibration.

The complete bridge was generally acknowledged to be a masterpiece: "the most colossal structure of the foremost industrial nation, standing as it does in a place where the natural scenery sets off its superb proportion ....". Opinions differed however concerning its beauty. William Morris observed "there never will be an architecture in iron; every improvement in machinery being uglier, until we reach the supremest specimen of all ugliness - the Forth Bridge". Sir Benjamin Baker's reply was masterly:

"Probably Mr Morris would judge the beauty of a design from the same standpoint whether it was for a bridge a mile long or for a silver chimney ornament. It is impossible for anyone to pronounce authoritatively on the beauty of an object without knowing its function. The marble columns of the Parthenon are beautiful where they stand but if we took one and bored a hole throught its axis and used it as a funnel of an Atlantic liner it would to my mind cease to be beautiful but of course Mr Morris might think otherwise". In this debate, The Times

inclined to Baker's point of view remarking that "Fortunately no attempt was made to decorate the bridge itself with flimsy adornments. It was allowed to stand out in simple and impressive grandeur".

On completion, the bridge became one of the wonders of the industrial world. The achievements of the engineers were conveniently indicated by the statistics of the bridge. It was 8,296 feet long. Each of the main spans was 1,710 feet long or 3.6 times as long as the Brittania Bridge over the Menai Straits, until then the longest span in Britain. The steel in the main spans weighed 51,000 tons, was held together by 8 million rivets and provided 145 acres of surface to paint. Besides there were 21,000 tons of cement, 47,000 of granite and 113,000 of other stone. When two trains together weighing 1,800 tons were brought to a halt on the bridge, the Board of Trade inspectors recorded a deflection never more than 7.6 inches. The true achievement however was more faithfully indicated by the immense technical advances made by its designers and builders. They pioneered the science of steel bridge - building by virtually creating a new technology.

North British tank engine 1879 designed by D. Drummond
It would have crossed the Forth Rail Bridge on local journeys.

CHAPTER VII

Village Resources

Inadequate detail exists to paint a full picture at a point in time. Consequently the aim in this chapter is to pick up topics whose origins may have been in previous periods and to follow these through to the end of the 19th century and beyond. So far we have implied that the village existed solely for the ferry, supplying the labour to run it and in return receiving sustenance, as if the be-all and end-all of the village was to carry out a single economic function. Nothing could be further from the truth. In reality the occupational pattern was complex, reflecting the availability of resources such as water, fertile land, marine life and dolerite rock.

Water

We are apt to forget how essential a local supply of water is to the development of communities. Without piped water, all requirements had to be carried by hand. It was important to site houses close to a well. Even then, the job of carrying water, which was allotted to the womenfolk, was an arduous one. The Inverkeithing Kirk session frequently admonished parishioners for carrying in water on the Sabbath, so presumably the elders expected double quantities to be brought in on Saturdays. Water was an important resource which had to be guarded from misuse or pollution, Simpson mentions four wells in the Cruickness, one of which was so near the high tide mark that it became unfit for use after very high tides. On one occasion a sailor was found washing his feet in it, to the indignation of local residents.

We may well have lost track of some of the old wells. We know that there was one near Ferrybarns Farm (ie near the support arches of the present Road Bridge) and another before reaching the ferry toll known as Lady Well. Another is shown on the 1854 Ordnance Survey map on Battery Road. When during a period of drought, the village wells ran dry, supplies were brought in from there. We know of three village wells. In all probability they are supplied from the freshwater loch in the

Ferryhills. The highest of these is at the bend in the road just below the Old School House. It is called the Jubilee Well because a stone has been erected there to commemorate Queen Victoria's diamond jubilee. The inscription reads "This ancient spring was restored by lovers of the Ferry for the solace of wayfarers and in memory of sixty years of Her Majesty's reign happily completed 1837-1897". On the wall, higher up the Brae the date 1783 is chiselled in the stone. At this point stood a water house, presumably built so that the villagers could control the use of their water supply. It was a small stone building and was in existence at least as late as the 1930's. From the records of North Queensferry Sailors' Society we know that there was a water committee. In July 1822 it borrowed £3 from the Sailors' Society "to be repaid in six months with interest". This was for "raising the walls and putting a lock on the well". Another entry in July 1850 tells us that Peter Bell a quarryman had approached John Anderson, who was employed to look after the well, in order to borrow the key to the well-house. He did so "to see what water was in it and now retains it; although repeatedly requested to return it, he refuses to do so". The Committee resolved "to use every legal means to get possession of the key".

We have already referred to Willie's Well. If a person was reluctant to leave the ferry it was said "ye maun hae drunk oot o' Willie's Well". This well was on the edge of land, known in the 17th century as the common green or strynd. The latter word means water spring. The green was used for bleaching. The well was restored in 1937. Brock says the water was very clear but that it was too hard for washing purposes. The main village well stood at the bottom of the Brae. It is still marked by two memorials. The lower is known as the Waterloo Well. It is built in rough stone and has the date 1816 on it, together with an indistinct representation of a passage boat. Below it a massive stone trough was recently found. This was used for watering the horses and washing down the coaches during the stage coach era. The trough has since been moved to the area next to the war memorial and regrettably is now used to deposit empty beer cans and litter. Above the Waterloo Well is a water tap in cast iron. The design, which incorporates a lion's head, is a common 19th century one. An identical tap

Lion's head water fountain

stood in Inverkeithing High Street. Above the North Queensferry well is a small cast-iron plaque which may have been made in an Inverkeithing foundry. The foundry was mentioned in the Old Statistical Account of Inverkeithing (1794) as making "beautiful chimney grates .... and all kinds of cast iron work for machinery and home utensils". The plaque has two pictures on it in bas relief. The first is of a nude woman on the back of a creature which has a bull's head and a sea monster's tail. This appears to represent the legend of Europa and the bull. The second shows a fully dressed woman in local costume. She wears an extremely tall hat and is fighting with a man. He is variously described as a foreign sailor or the caretaker of the well. The first of these descriptions seems the more likely. Foreign vessels often lay wind-bound in St Margaret's Hope. Their crews landed for water and provisions and in times of drought they may have constituted a threat to the local community. Because the Summer supply of water was uncertain, this well had a lock put on it. Every day at a regular hour a waterman opened the well; the women queuing to take their turn at the well. In the 1880's piped water from Glensherup reached the village so that in due course this daily ritual would have died out. Nevertheless in the early 20th century the village still had a waterman responsible for its wells and for street lighting. Even latterly water was not widely available. Many cottages had water piped in for cooking purposes but no bath room or internal lavatory.

Farming

What with the spread of houses, the growth of quarries and the immense cuttings in connection with the Road Bridge and the railway line, little is left of the Ferryhills. The modern observer must wonder that there was any room for farming. In fact there were three farms on the ferry peninsula; Ferrybarns, Cruicks and Carlingnose. In 1872 Ballingall found the land behind the village "fertile, well-cultivated and beautifully diversified". Only one of the farmhouses survives: Carlingnose. The present farmhouse, now converted to a dwelling appears to be an 18th century building. In the period 1830-35 it was described as a "wretched old farm house .... a building which seems to have been erected when agriculture was at a low ebb". Nevertheless the Ferryhills were "clothed in the finest pasture .... covered with horses, cattle and sheep". At this time too the farmhouse was used only as a dwelling but later in the 19th century we know it was a farm from a plan of the steading dated 1886.

The area now occupied by St Margaret's Place, Whinny Knowe, and Brock Street is shown in an early 19th century map as pasture and arable land. Within living memory the land above the school was known as the stubble fields. The same map shows "old barn and stack yard" on the site of the Old School House. Our picture of local agriculture is somewhat lacking in detail. For a picture of sheep rearing on the Ferryhills we turn to Brock's papers. In Autumn 1929 he was watching the training of a new sheep dog on the

Lamp standard 'over the Old Road', originally for gas, now converted for electricity. The last village lamp lighter was George Donaldson

Carlinquose Farm

ferry hills and his notes read as follows:

10th Sept. 1929   Shepherd (WILL HAY)
  on golfcourse
Training new dog; patience needed.
Rounding up sheep for counting; one
  sheep lame with foot-rot; hoof to
  be cut away and dressed with "foot-
  rot dressing" (carbolic and
  arsenic)
These sheep 18 months old; to be
  killed in next few weeks; does
  not pay to keep longer.
One fleece (10 lbs) should cover
  cost of keep for one year (4½d -
  6d per week). Wool sells at
  1/6 per lb.
Wool and mutton both coarsen with
  age; therefore best to kill at
  18 months or so.
Some sheep kept for wool. One
  crossbred Sussex Down in flock;
  finer wool.
Sheep's age known by teeth.
Muggy weather at present bad
  for maggot.
Young dog shy; has probably been
  badly used in breaking; will
  not come close or lie down.
Breeding ewes aged sometimes
  10 years - 9 pairs of lambs.
Young dog taken on leash, while
  old dog works.

In another part of Brocks papers we learn that
in the 1870's a number of dairymen from
Inverkeithing kept their cattle on the Ferry
hills and also raised crops of corn, turnip
and potatoes to feed them. Each holder
employed a herd laddie who besides looking after
the cattle was responsible for selling the milk.
The herd laddie got his keep plus 3 to 4 shillings
per week. At the end of the season a "Herd's

race" was held at which the prizes were:

1) a pair of trousers
2) a pair of drawers
3) a shirt
4) a pair of braces
5) a pair of socks.

Fishing

The village is bounded on three sides by water.
Moreover up to the early 20th century this water
was rich in marine life of all sorts. For
instance the Old Statistical Account for South
Queensferry mentions cod, haddock, whiting, skate,
flounder, herring, crab, lobster and oysters.
Such abundant food close at hand would have
made a considerable difference to health and
standards of living, bearing in mind that in
former times protein was rarely available in
adequate quantities, at least not to ordinary
folk. Besides, local inhabitants were well-
equipped as sailors and sea-farers to exploit
this local resource.

We know that fishermen inhabited the coasts of
the River Forth in prehistoric times. In other
parts of the estuary piles of shells have been
found and also the remains of a whale beside
which a prehistoric bone tool was found. There
is no reason to suppose that the whale remains
found under a house in the old village date
from this time, but we do know that local residents
were fishermen and even whale hunters.

Malcolm IV granted "to the Abbot of Dunfermline
and to the monks serving God there .... the
heads of the fishes which are called Crespeis
except the tongue, which may be stranded in my
lordship by that part of Scotwater (ie Forth) in
which part their church stands". Crespeis is
thought to be short for crassus pisces, denoting
some sort of whale or large porpoise. Apparently

the tongues of these animals were considered a delicacy, for the King claimed these as his own. The rest went to the monks and was used for food and fuel, the blubber being used amongst other things as oil for altar lights. There are numerous instances of whales climbing the Forth either to be stranded on the Fife or Lothian shores or to climb still further up river. For instance Sibbald relates that an 80' whale was stranded on the Fife coast in 1652. Its jaws were later taken to make a garden gate at Pitfirrane House. More interesting to our local history, one was actually captured off North Queensferry in July 1843. The whale was sighted a quarter of a mile from the North Queensferry passage. The ferry Superintendent and the boatmen

of the station were quickly on the alert. They put out in their boats and succeeded in striking several harpoons in the whale's back. Chalmers continues "The scene now presented peculiar interest .... the whale at one time darting from his assailants, at another throwing volumes of water into the air, while he lashed the water with his tail .... The contest lasted for some time but in about an hour the whale being weakened by his continued efforts and great loss of blood, victory was declared on the side of the boatmen who then towed the huge monster of the deep on shore". There, it was measured and found to be 51' long and 19' 9" in circumference. Whales were frequently sighted. Another which arrived off North Queensferry in February 1857 and stayed for a month, was a great deal luckier. It got ample food from shoals of garvies (a kind of sprat about 5-5½ " long which resembles a young herring) and was unharmed by the many shots fired at it including several from the cannon of the "Chieftain" man-of-war which was stationed above the ferry at the time.

Garvies are still frequent visitors to the Forth. They ascend the river as the weather turns colder and arrive here in sufficient numbers to make a commercial catch in mid-February. Other species no longer venture into these polluted waters. Salmon were common as late as 1890. Some managed to enter the steel caissons used to build the stone supports of the railway bridge. Stake nets were erected at Port Laing and at the entrance of Inverkeithing harbour to catch them. Herring were a far more important visitor. An early Privy Council decree (1587) forbade the export of herring. Inverkeithing magistrates were "to arreist and stay all and quatsumevir schippis and veschillis already laden with the said herring". The Old Statistical Account

for South Queensferry mentions that in 1792 large numbers of herring arrived in the Forth outside Inverkeithing Bay. Boats from ports as far away as Burntisland and Boness fished there. Some herring boats even came from the West side of the country via the Forth Clyde Canal. It was estimated that almost every day 80-100 boats were busily and successfully employed fishing for herring. A single boat might come in with 30 or 40 barrels selling at £8 - £10 each. About 6,000 barrels were cured in South Queensferry in a year. At North Queensferry things were done on a smaller scale. Heron House on the East side of the old village was known earlier as Herring House and this was where the fish were cured. (Similarly Helen Place may be a corruption of herring). There would also have been employment for fish wives. Dick gives us a picture of their work. The herring were thrown, into troughs. The gutters wore big boots and tarpaulin aprons, their fingers tied with bandages to protect them from cuts. "Holding a sharp pointed knife in the right hand they seize a herring in their left; one jerk and the knife is inserted above the gills and the contents wrenched away, the fish deftly thrown into one of three different tubs according to size. They handle 20-30 fish a minute." The fish were salted and packed in barrels. They were then allowed to stand for a day. Then more fish were packed into the barrel before it was closed. Finally brine was poured in at the bung hole until no more could be absorbed. Then the barrels were ready for despatch. Such activity would have been commonplace in the village in the early 19th century.

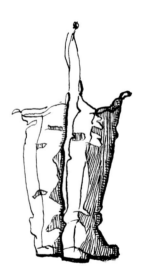

By 1836 the local herring industry had all but disappeared: the herring went as mysteriously as they came. But there were still plentiful supplies of other varieties. Cunningham and Brock both refer to the landing of catches at North Queensferry in the late 19th century. On such mornings the village was thronged with cadgers' carts, sometimes stretching right down the Main Street and back along the side of the West Bay. They would go down on to the beach to buy their supplies (the slipway behind the Albert Hotel is still known by some as Cadgers' Pier). Having collected their fish they would race out of the village to the surrounding towns and villages so that they would get a good price before more plentiful supplies should reach the market. At this time villagers could go down to the pier to buy fish at between 1d and 6d per bowl depending on quantity; others fished to pay the November rent. Fishing boats put in at the Ferry well into the 20th century but more infrequently. At this time the village was supplied by fish sellers such as Herrin Davie and Mary Scrougie from Inverkeithing and Ellen Fairnie from Cockenzie. The latter came by train. She carried her fish in a basket on her back which was secured with a strap around the forehead.

Another important marine resource was sea-weed. This was used, and still is used, directly as fertiliser. Alternatively it could be turned into kelp. Simson tells us that it was collected on the East shore of the peninsula. We know from other sources that "the sea ware" was collected all along the shore by the adjacent farmers. It was cut by means of a reaping hook. As the tide rose, it floated and was pulled ashore with a rope. It was "burned in a round stone circle of moderate height; when the residue after being puddled by iron rods, became the kelp of commerce". This was then converted into potash or iodine. We find from the Guildry records of Dunfermline that in July 1768 John Craig, bleacher in Linlithgow proposed "to take the fishings at North Queensferry opposite to the Guildry's lands, for a term of years". The Guildry gave him a 40 year tack for 40/- yearly rent. Seven years later the Dean of Guild was authorised "to lett the sea-ware at ye ferry .... for this year's cutting only by publick roup .... and ye roup to be intimate at Dunfermline Kirk doors Sunday next and through ye town by ye drum on ye market day and yer lett to be made for ready money only". They accepted an offer from James Cunningham, vintner in North Ferry "to enter into tack with the Guildry for the whole of ye subjects at North Ferry, houses, land and sea ware". The rent was £57 per annum and the tack was for 19 years.

To conclude this section on fish and fishing we turn to Brock's beautiful account of herring fishing outside Inverkeithing Bay in the 1930's: "Finally an unforgettable view is that presented on a clear mild winter night when the little herring fleet is fishing a short distance off-shore in the lee of the ferry hills. The boats, motor yawls, lie perhaps some 30 or 40 of them in a rough arc of a circle with the convex side shorewards. Their bright lights, yellow, red and green, produce long tremulous reflections in the water. Here and there a boat moves about among the others, altering its position. The fishermen work quietly and hardly anything is heard save the rhythmic splashing of the tide on Port Laing beach, the occasional muffled sound of a train crossing the Bridge. The moon has perhaps not yet risen over Dunearn Hill and the sky is jewelled with countless stars contrasting in their steely brilliance with the more homely yellow lights of the fishing yawls. These boats will be seen lying there at any hour during the night but as the hours lengthen out towards morning they gradually

work further afield and at daybreak they disperse to land their catches at various points in the Firth".

Quarrying

Brock, writing in the early 1930's noted that quarrying was then the single most important source of local employment. This was probably true throughout the previous century and a half. The first we hear of quarrying is in 1763 when Robert Campbell, a Stirling merchant "compeared and desired liberty of quarrying of whin stones for the London casway within the floodmark opposite to the Guildry's new barn, near the Haugh end by West the town". The Guildry gave him permission for "the quarrying and dressing of stones for casway laying". The grant extended "from the East March of that part of the Guildry's lands by West the said North Ferrie, to the point of the rocks jutting into the sea, a little by West the said new Barn". This is the part of the coast on either side of the approach arches of the present road bridge. This venture must have turned out well because the next year Campbell asked for permission to quarry "by East" the village. The Guildry owned most of Castlehill (beneath the present railway bridge). They agreed to him quarrying, but not more than 400 yards from the floodmark. His tack was for 8 years on the East side of the village. The scale of his operations must have been pretty large, for one of the conditions of the tack was that he was to pay an increased rent if he ever employed more than 106 men. In the same year we learn that he encroached on land belonging to neighbouring proprietors. Three years later he was employing 39 men "over and above the hundred and six men allowed by the tack as constant men" and had not notified the Guildry of the fact. He had paid a rent of £37 in the previous year, not allowing for overmanning (which was at the rate of 4/- per annum per extra man) or for the damage he had caused to arable land. Campbell's operations on the East of the village appear to have been at

Illustrations : Nineteenth century wheelbarrow, sea boots and lantern.

Quarry and Kingscroft

locations marked on the 1854 map on either side of the present signal station.

In 1775 William Ross a retired soldier and a married man who had lost his eyesight working in a quarry at North Queensferry applied to the Kirk session of Inverkeithing "to get interest made for him to be admitted a Blue Gown". Blue gowns were a class of beggars authorised by the sovereign who became the sovereign's bedesmen. In return for alms they were supposed to pray for the welfare of the sovereign and the country. Blue gowns wore a pewter badge with the Crown and the words "Pass and Repass" embossed on it. They were equipped with a gown, a hood, shoes, a wooden cup and platter, and a purse containing one shilling Scots for each year of the sovereign's reign. These authorised beggars often frequented Inverkeithing where the Kirk session gave them sums ranging from one shilling to 6/8d. The Kirk session brought the case of Ross to the notice of an influential churchman. In due course he was admitted to the order.

The 1854 Ordnance Survey map reveals seven quarries on the Queensferry peninsula. Six of these yielded the volcanic rock dolerite known locally as whinstone and the seventh, the Welldean quarry provided free-stone. Whinstone was in considerable demand from the 18th century onwards as slabs, sets and kerbs for use in pavements, roads, harbours and other public works. The local deposits are particularly rich (indeed the peninsula is practically solid dolerite) and the location close to sea transport was immensely advantageous considering the weight of the commodity. We learn that the local stone was used in the construction of the Forth Clyde canal, Leith docks, London pavements, Liverpool docks and Cronstadt harbour fortifications. Pennant toured Scotland in the 1770's and recorded his impressions. He termed the local rock "granite". He noticed that it lay in "great perpendicular stacks above which is a reddish earth filled with micaceous modules. The granite itself is very hard and is all blasted with gun-powder; the cutting into shape for paving costs two shillings and eight pence per tun and the freight to London seven shillings". He noted that several vessels

were moored near the village in order to take their lading.

The new statistical account (1836) notes that the local stone was used for building, roadmaking and paving but that "the granite of Aberdeen is now preferred for the latter purpose". This may have been the case, but quarrying still provided a great deal of local employment. Ferry Toll quarry originated in the early 18th century. It was now joined by the Welldean quarry, and later by the Jubilee quarry, the stone being shipped from all of these from a wharf near the present motorway roundabout. Stephen dates the Carlingnose quarry at 1838 and the Cruicks quarry (the only quarry still in existence) ten years earlier. The former is clearly indicated on the 1854 map. Two tram roads are shown for transporting the stone, most of which was shipped from a wharf immediately beneath Carlingnose. The remains of the wharf are still in existence. Some of these quarries fell into disuse in the late 19th century but the advent of the internal combustion engine seems to have been their salvation by creating a demand for road-metalling. In the early 20th century the Tilbury company reopened the Welldean and Ferry Toll quarries, and opened the Lucknow quarry on the Cruicks peninsula. At the same time Messrs Bruntons, quarrymasters commenced operations on the inland portion of the Castle-hill. The result is the present quarry hole on the East of the railway bridge. The neat row of houses nearby now known as Forthview Terrace housed the quarry workmen and was then known disparagingly as Bug Row. Priory Cottage housed the overseer and in 1902 Brunton's Hall was opened to provide a social centre for the quarrymen and villagers. This was the scene of many dances, entertainments and parties. It is remembered by older residents with a mixture of affection and sadness in view of its present condition.

Thus at the beginning of the 20th century two quarries were being worked close to the centre of the village; the Carlingnose and Battery quarries. Many of the quarrymen came from Inverkeithing. They worked a ten hour day (6.00 am to 5.00 pm with an hour for lunch) for which labourers were paid £1 per week and blacksmiths, who sharpened the tools, £1-10-0. It was a 6 day week with no Saturday afternoons off. The quarrymen were paid monthly but were able to get a line of credit at the shop from the foreman. The quarrymen's children brought them breakfast at 9.00 am of "porridge in pitchers tied up in napkins". Those coming from Inverkeithing came over the Old Road stopping at the dairy (now Garthhill) to pick up milk. Some were chased by the ferry boys with whom there was keen rivalry. Brock records the following taunt:

> Inverkeithing beagles lockit in a box
>
> Canna get ower the door for the ferry game cocks

William Duff of Rosyth lived in the Ferry at the beginning of this century, worked in both the Battery and Carlingnose quarries and is the last known kerb-dresser in Fife. The methods and tools he used, would have been more or less the same over several hundred years, at least until the earlier part of this century. Then with the arrival of the motor car, and the growing popularity of concrete as a cheap and versatile substitute for cut-stone, these methods changed. In the late 19th century for instance the local quarries produced only sets and kerbs. Then in the early 20th century they experienced a growing demand for road metal. To produce this the stone was fed into crushers and then screened in order to sort it into the required sizes. At the Carlingnose large hoppers were installed, the remains of which are still visible on the screes above St James Bay. The stone was fed into these and taken off below to load into small steam vessels and occasionally into sailing vessels. Brock notes that in the thirties the Cruicks Quarry had eleven crushers in operation, producing road metal for export to England. It was loaded on steamers of 400-800 tons which ran regularly to English ports. The cost of conveying the stone by water round the North of Scotland to Manchester was only 10 to 12 shillings per ton. The LNER however, could not quote a charge less than 19 to 20 shillings per ton.

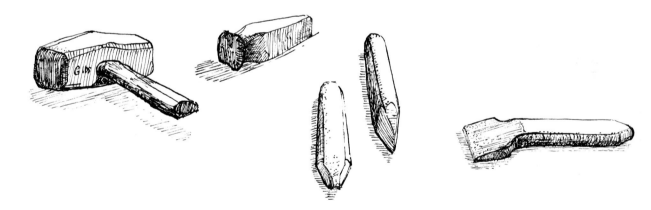

Selection of quarrying tools.

CHAPTER VIII

A Way of Life

How did the inhabitants of North Queensferry live in former times?   Having already looked at the way they earned their living, this remains one of the most difficult questions to answer.

The 1851 census gives us an idea.   In the whole Ferryhills peninsula there were 593 persons, of whom 279 were male and 314 female.   The number of inhabited houses was 85.   Thus the average occupancy was 7.1 persons per house.   In the village proper there were 357 persons of whom 44 per cent were aged 19 or below.   The average age of villagers was only 27 and the structure through the age groups as follows:

| Age | Percent in each age group | |
	Male	Female
Under 10 years	26	28
10-19	18	16
20-29	14	16
30-39	14	11
40-49	12	11
50-59	9	8
60-69	3	7
70 and above	4	3

Clearly the population was a very young one with very marked representation in the early age groups and very small numbers of aged.   The oldest man was aged 82 and the only male octogenarian.   The oldest women were 84 and 85 respectively.

The census mentions 114 occupations.   The single most important source of employment was quarry-working which accounted for 40 of the 114.   The other important source of livelihood was the sea which collectively accounted for another 30 occupations as follows:

Ships carpenters	6
Sailors	4
Boatmen (customs, coast-guards)	6
Ferry boatmen	4
Ferry porter	1
Steamboat engineer	1
Fishermen	8
	30

The small extent of employment on the ferry reflects the recent opening of the Granton-Burntisland route to the North and the consequent decline in importance of the Queensferry.

Cot with doll,
nineteenth century

A large number of skills, crafts and livelihoods are mentioned:

grocers	2
vintners	3
dealer in small wares	1
baker, dairyman and carter	1
postmistress	1
tailors	2
laundresses	3
shoemakers	2
dressmakers	2
sick nurse	1
teacher	1
constable	1

Of those without gainful employment, a large number of scholars are mentioned, and 18 paupers,

The Sailors' Society

The burial records of North Queensferry Sailors' Society are another useful source of information about village life. They are now kept by the Department of Leisure, Recreation and Amenities of Dunfermline District Council, who besides invigorating the living, bring comfort to the dead in the capacity of keepers of local grave-yards. The Sailors' Society was a type of friendly society the object of which was to provide for the decent burial of deceased members and of certain non-members. The latter were charged a fee for the mort-cloth and burial plot. There were two classes of members: proprietors and ordinary members. The families of the former were allotted a plot in the burial ground, (this being the ruins of St James Chapel which stands in the centre of the old village whose grounds were levelled by bringing sand from the fore shore). The grounds were then divided into two portions: the New Ground contained 60 plots; the Old Ground 48 plots.

Burial ground in the ruins of St James Chapel

15 of whom were women. The following street names are mentioned:

Main road

East road

Chapel road

Fore close

Back close

Ure's close

Peaceable land

North road

Finally, we notice that the population of the village even at this early stage was in a state of flux. For instance, of 170 males in the village proper, 101 were incomers born outside North Queensferry. In the adult group the importance of outsiders is even more marked. Of 96 males of 20 years or above living in the village, 69 had been born elsewhere.

We find, for instance, that Alexander Seggie had 3 breadths (Nos. 1, 2 and 3): that Robert Millions also had three (Nos. 18, 19 and 20) and that James Brown of the Brae had only 2 breadths (Nos 37 and 38), the last-mentioned being President of the Sailors' Society. Ordinary members paid a reduced fee for membership and paid less than non-members for burial and use of the Society's mort cloths.

The Society had existed in the 18th century but had been dissolved. In October 1818 the former members resolved "to constitute themselves anew and invite their neighbours to join them in the laudable design". The rules of the previously existing Society were adopted. These had fixed the entry money for those without birth rights (ordinary members) at 20/-, but the meeting resolved that the entry fee should be only 10/6d, until the funds of the Society were stronger. This was a sensible step because although the Society was "not indebted to any whatsoever", it had funds of £2-10-0. Moreover with only 16 members whose "salaries" (subscriptions) were fixed at 1/- per half year, the financial situation was precarious. The meeting elected office bearers as follows:

James Brown (Brae)	Preses
John Ellis	Box master
John McRitchie	Key keeper
John Inglis	Clerk
William Greig	Officer

These were supported by a committee of six, with the sensible result that most of the Society's members were either officers or committee members. The meeting resolved to collect the outstanding debts of the former Sailors' Society which "shall be carefully collected and deposited in the box". Moreover those having occasion for the mort cloths or ground of the Society would be charged a fee by the Clerk who would keep a cash book recording the transactions.

Two years later the membership had increased to 26 and the funds of the Society stood at £15-18-0. Most of the Society's money was lodged at the Dunfermline Savings Bank but some was advanced on loan to John Ellis and Alexander Seggie who paid the Society interest. The practice of advancing money to villagers on loan was later to give the Society trouble. Despite the financial improvement some strain was felt. Consequently in December 1821 the entry money was reduced to 5/- "and also for the strengthening of the box .... The box shall be shut for the space of twelve months". In addition the salary was increased to 1/- per quarter. At a meeting in 1831 it was noted that "many of the inhabitants have burying grounds in the chapel but are not members and do not contribute to the upkeep of the walls etc". Accordingly fees were fixed as follows for use of the Society's mort-cloths:

Non-members who are proprietors

8/- large

4/- small

Non-members who are not proprietors

6/- large

3/- small

There are numerous examples of the Sailors' Society administering a primitive form of social security. For instance, the charges noted above were agreed "with power of the committee to grant abatement where the poverty of the relatives may require it". In addition throughout the burial records, certain deaths are marked "gratis":

"September 30th - John McQueen, travelling
1832   packsman - ground and
         cloth gratis"

Moreover in making its expenditure the Society often got work done by those in greatest need. Colin Reid who died in 1839 ("upwards of 90 years of age") had been frequently employed cleaning the chapel yard. In 1820, with the village facing starvation, the Society paid £10 to its committee "to be applied for the purpose of supplying the village with meal at as reasonable rate as possible". The money was repaid in

the Summer of the same year. In 1822 the village water committee borrowed money from the Society for "raising the walls and putting a door on the well". In 1839 "William Blake, a member being in indigence rec'd £1 til next meeting" and three years later the committee resolved to give one pound each to two "old and decayed members .... and their causes to be further considered at the June meeting".

The main business of the Society however, was burials and these are recorded in "A List of the Dead Buried in the Chappel or Chappel Yard this year of our Lord 1812". Many of the deaths were the result of accidents at sea. For instance:

"David Bell had his leg Brok coming tou
in a Pinnas and it was cut off and he Died
Tousday ye 12 Day of May and was buried"

A similar fate befell John Seggy who in 1814 "Got his lig Brook on Board of the .... (illegible) and died". For breaking a leg to prove fatal, medical aids must have been primitive or non existent. Several deaths from drowning are recorded:

"William Spence Drowned along with all
the crew and the vessel lost on the East
Coast 11th October" 1823

"David McRitchie Drowned in Well Dean
Quarry 22 April and the body found
19 May" 1823

David McRitchie junior succeeded his deceased father as a member of the Sailors' Society. Calling the son by the father's christian name appears to have been common. Five years later the Society membership included

two William Andersons   (Junior and Senior)

two Charles Roxburghs   "   "   "

three David McRitchies

One of the latter identified as living on the Brae, drowned in 1833. In November 1830 John McRitchie had drowned and in those three years two others also met the same fate.

The most pathetic aspect of the burial ground records is the premature death of children (far more common in the 19th century than it is today) and the multiple deaths of families.

In 1826 of the 8 deaths recorded 5 were children. At that time we have the following entries:

October 27	1826	James Cairn's child
November 1	1827	" " "
10	1828	" " stillborn child
16	"	Another child of the above James Cairns

In April 1837 we have

| April 8 | Janet Braugh, wife of Sam Chisholm, member. |
| 16 | William Chisholm aged 5, son of Sam Chisholm |

and two years later:

| October 26 | Sam Chisholm. |

By far the most disturbing series of entries, perhaps indicative of some unrecorded epidemic, are the following consecutive entries in 1879-80 all of which relate to children:

1879	February	Elizabeth Harvey	2 years 7 months
	June	William Brown	6 years
1880	January	John Browne Sharpe	6 years
	January	James Sime	4 days
	June	Sharak Shaw	17 days
	September	Peter, son of Peter Moodie	8 months
	October	Finlay Duff	6 months
		Magdalene Harvey	15 months
		Hugh Grant Cameron	7 weeks

Such a record must for ever dispel the notion that life in former times was romantic. On the contrary it was characterised, as Hobbes put it, by "continual fear and danger of violent death and the life of man was solitary, poor, nasty, brutish and short".

For deliverance from such tribulations some will thank the Lord; others the marvels of modern technology. Whatever the cause, let us be thankful we were born in the 20th century.

Before leaving the Sailors' Society let us look at some of its expenditure. In 1818 we have

To the clerk, coal and candle	1/6d
To the officer warning the meeting	1/-
To Jas. Thomson, repairing Chapel gate	6d
To Wm. Blake clearing Chapel ground	4/-

In 1821 "It was resolved that a Crier's hand bell should be purchased as the property of the Society and at any meeting said Bell shall be given in charge to a proper person (a Member in preference) he paying yearly to the Society what shall be thought a reasonable sum". The bell cost 10/- and the reasonable sum started at 2/- and rose to 3/6 by 1839. Money was also spent on the burial ground

| Robert Malcolme, 12 days repairing Chappel dyke | £1-4-0 |
| Robert Fraiter, Lime, sand, stones, carriage | £0-14-0 |

Apparently certain members were also allowed a

funeral allowance:

| May 21 1824 | Paid Dad McRitchie Senr. funeral allowance for wife | £1-10-0 |
| | Paid Dad McRitchie Junr. funeral allowance for father | £2-00-0 |

The Committee was careful in making the proper disbursements:

| December 1830 | To paid Jas Macgregor's funeral money of Willm Spense a member who died at Dundee deducting 5/- being five quarters salary due to Society at his death | £1-15-0 |

In 1846 the funeral allowances were increased to £5 for a member and £3 for a member's wife.

By 1839 the funds of the Society were quite substantial, totalling £80-8-6d. Some of this money was held on deposit but the bulk had been lent to several villagers who acknowledged their debts to the Society via bills of exchange. One of these to James W Ritchie amounted to £50. In 1848 we hear that correspondence regarding Mrs McRitchie's bill was laid on the table and the meeting agreed to allow Mr Fraser to proceed against the parties for the amount of the bill. Later that year a preventive measure was taken: all other bill holders were required to pay their bills within 3 days after date.

The village school

There is a strong link between the village school and the Sailors' Society. In 1769 the Society acquired a house known as Malinkie Cottage for use as a school. This has since been demolished but stood at the East end of Helen Place, on the South side where there are now steps and a vacant lot. It was in this house that the Sailors' Society held many of its meetings. Part was

Illustrations :   Tomb stones in the Sailors' Society burial grounds used as a school, the other part being rented out:

"Oct 19 1832   Received from Widow Chapman
                part of 30/- of rent of old
                school, due at Martinmas"

The Sailors' Society was responsible for the upkeep of the building:

1818	"To Alexr Garden glazing school windows	10/-"
1823	"To allowance, whitening the school, coal and candle	2/-"
1824	"Plaistering school	3/3d."

The frequent need to reglaze the school windows seems to indicate a degree of vandalism.   Anyway the building was dilapidated so a plan was made to establish "a respectable school house in the village of North Queensferry".   Captain McConochie seems to have been one of the guiding influences behind the scheme.   He persuaded the local land owners to subscribe £100.   The Inverkeithing Council added £30 and the Guildry of Dunfermline also subscribed.   The Sailors' Society "agreed that twenty pounds be given in aid of this important object in the name of North Ferry Sailors' Society and that we shall endeavour to promote a general subscription in the village".

The result was the building we now call the Old School House situated half way up the Brae near the Jubilee Well.   Over the door on the South side is the bell, which the dominie rang to summon the children to their lessons.   Behind it, chiselled in the stone are the words: "Built by public subscription AD 1827".   It is this building that Simson refers to as being recently built.   He describes it as having a schoolroom on the ground floor and the teacher's dwelling above, the latter being entered by a stairway on the north side.   Simson's recollections relate mostly to his school days at Inverkeithing.   He remarks that in Summertime about half of the children went to school barefoot. Presumably this would have been the same at North Queensferry.

In 1829 Munro Ross Esq of Rosshill (the large property by Dalmeny Station) bequeathed £200 to the trustees of the Ferry Passage "to be lent on good security or to be laid out in the purchase of heritable property and mortified for ever". The income was to be used to promote the education of boys born in the village (an early example of sexual prejudice!) and was to be spent "in providing books, paper, pens and ink, for them to be taken in at the age of six years and remain at school four years, and preference to be given to boys whose parents or other relatives were under me in military service" (Mr Ross was in command of the North Queensferry volunteers during the Napoleonic War).   The boys were to be taught "reading, writing, arithmetic and book-keeping or other branches of education".

About the same time the ferrymen decided to stop the schoolmaster's salary which as we have seen was paid from the ferry takings.   Why they did this, is unclear.   Captain McConochie advised them "to resume their subscription towards the support of their old schoolmaster whose active services they have commanded above thirty years and which under all circumstances it is a shame for them as men and as parents ever to have suspended".   The schoolmaster who suffered this

treatment was John Inglis, another North Queensferry volunteer.   Indeed it was he who had written the volunteers' offer of military service in 1797.

Door of the Old School House.

Nicholson sheds light on the school and one of its more interesting occupants at this time. A "second schoolmaster" who had lost the lower part of one leg, had a wooden stump with which to walk.   He detached this at will and used it as a dibble when tending his garden.   He was also fond of breakfast.   After his wife's death a lad was sent down the Brae each morning to fetch him a hot plate of porridge.   A picturesque character indeed!   But we must wonder at his ability to teach English because when confronted with misbehaviour, he is reported to have exclaimed "If ye dinna behave yersels Ill gie ye a guff a' lug and kick ye doon a' brae".   Nicholson notes the diminutive size of the Old School House and the irony of a contemporary reference which describes it as "a large and commodious school".   He adds that in the period 1830-40 it was used out of school hours for prayer meetings.

The Old School House has the unusual distinction of having been administered first by the trustees of the Queensferry Passage and then for eleven years until 1874 by the North British Railway Co. The railway company's undertaking concerning the school house is contained in an Act of Parliament of 1863.   This acknowledges the residue of the legacy left by Captain Ross (£80) and provides that the company "shall hold the said schoolhouse upon and for the same trusts, ends and purposes and under the same conditions and obligations as before .... and shall pay interest half yearly at the rate of five pounds per centum per annum to the schoolmaster of North Queensferry".   In 1874 management of the school passed to Inverkeithing School Board.   With admirable speed the Board built a new school which was completed in 1876 for the sum of £546-6-0.   It was a one storey building which stood adjacent to the existing Old School House. The school house itself was repaired and altered. The cost of this was about £100, the sums being found by the Board borrowing £600 from the government and receiving a government grant of £165. In 1897 further space was provided by building a second storey to the new school at a cost of £1,000.

The population of the village was expanding. The 1901 census gave a total of 760 of whom 170 were of school age. By 1910 there were 191 on the roll and school accommodation for only 192. Luckily absentees averaged 8 per cent, but they were sometimes as little as 3 per cent. What with the new families brought in by men serving with the Royal Engineers (who were constructing the Carlingnose Fort) and the families to be expected once it was garrisoned, the time had come to look for larger premises. The result was the Primary School as we know it today. It was built for 300 pupils at a cost of £3,600 "having a whinstone front". A pressed brick front would have cost £30 less, but luckily funds ran to the use of the local stone.

Before leaving the village school, let us bring the record more up to date with extracts from the headmaster's log book.

10 October 1934	Fire drill carried out. Building evacuated in 28 seconds.
14 December 1934	HMI report "owing to changing local conditions the roll of this school has been falling markedly .... from 162 in 1931 to 109 in 1934 .... A section of the local population is migratory and during the past year more than half of the pupils on the roll left school"
8 February 1935	The "milk in school" scheme of the Milk Marketing Board has been in operation since Monday .... Attendance is greatly improved".
6 December 1935	Fire Drill: 31 seconds
1 April 1936	Fire Drill: 25 seconds
4 November 1936	New Headmaster
2 February 1937	Fire Drill - all pupils walking - 40 seconds.
11 May 1937	All pupils assembled in the gym where an address was read by the headmaster from the Secretary of State for Scotland. A souvenir coronation shilling was distributed to each child.
29 September 1938	Gas masks were distributed this afternoon to all children on the roll and to adults in the evening.
18 October 1938	Fire drill in 34 seconds "the children acting calmly and promptly".
25 August 1939	"A detachment of Cameron Highlanders occupied this school this afternoon"
28 August 1939	"The school which was to open this morning was not available owing to military occupation"
4 September 1939	"Owing to outbreak of war, school will remain closed for indefinite period".
13 October 1939	"Military remain in complete control of this school"
16 October 1939	"Air raid attack by German planes on ships near Forth Bridge. Request for evacuation renewed".
27 October 1939	35 registered evacuees medically examined and sent to Saline and Steelend.
9 November 1942	The school was reopened but found to be damaged by military occupation. "The stock rooms are both in a deplorable state and books are scattered in all directions".
30 April 1942	Organised games were begun in the Barracks field by permission of the Commanding Officer of the Battery.
17 May 1943	Removal of school railings to help the war effort.
10 May 1945	School reopened today after two days holidays following cessation of hostilities with Germany.
4 February 1946	Agreement to instal electric light.
13 December 1950	Representatives of the Architect's Department, Cupar agreed to instal electric light.
8 February 1952	The whole school was assembled in the drill hall to hear the proclamation of Queen Elizabeth.
8 June 1955	HMI Report "The premises which have recently been fitted with electric light .... the pupils were being taught with care and enthusiasm".

4 September 1964	School closed today for the opening of the Forth Road Bridge. Fifty pupils accompanied by staff attended the ceremony at the Northern Access to the Bridge.
17 June 1975	School outing in the village "The children showed great interest in the Little Houses and the marriage lintels".

Visitors

For a place of its size North Queensferry has always had a disproportionately large number of visitors, many of them birds of passage, involuntarily at Queensferry, before continuing to a more distant destination. For instance, a typical year in the 1960's would have seen 40,000 ferry boat crossings carrying:

1¼ million passengers
600,000 cars
200,000 commercial vehicles

In this section we are concerned with more permanent visitors. It is little appreciated that in the 19th century the village was a busy holiday resort. This was before this part of the Forth became dangerous to bathe in because of sewage and industrial waste. Before the building of the Railway Pier (1878) the Inner Bay was clean and sandy and therefore suitable for picnics and bathing. After this date the new pattern of the currents resulted in the build-up of unwholesome sludge which can be seen at low tide today. Fyffe tells us that at South Queensferry, when the ladies go for a swim, "the gentlemen willingly move off to a greater distance so that no misunderstanding can occur". We hope that behaviour was just as seemly here. In 1899 we are told that in Summer the normal population was "considerably augmented by sea bathers as summer lodgers are termed by the natives".

Summer visitors would find a boarding house or rent a cottage. Lothian, in his "Banks of the Forth" (1862) tells us that comfortable accommodation could be had in Burns Cottage, Braehouse, Ferryhouse, Seabank Cottage, North Cliff Cottages, Craig Cottages and Cruicks House. Ballingall, ten years later, describes North Queensferry as "a small village with a harbour, inhabited by a sprinkling of fisherman and a few boatmen employed on the station". Reid, in his "Tourist Guide to the Firth of Forth" (1876) mentions "good summer quarters are obtainable .... and a pleasant day may be spent by pleasure seekers". Twelve years later Beveridge describes it as "a pleasant and picturesque looking village". Even as late as 1899 a local shop advertised "List of houses to let. Enquirers please state requirements". Rev Wilson maintained that the village had a "healthy bracing character. Few places in Scotland can show a lower death rate among children and consumption is practically unknown among the resident population. The late Sir James Simpson to whom the world owes the use of chloroform in surgery, was, we believe, in the habit of sending patients to recover at North Queensferry. With medical climatologists, it is an accepted maxim that the vegetation of any

district affords a very reliable guide to its healthiness, and there are not many places in Scotland where wild flowers are to be found in greater variety and luxuriance than on the Ferryhills." (Cunningham 1899)

Other visitors came to the ferry peninsula for a different type of convalescence. These were the crew and passengers of vessels coming to the Forth, suspected of carrying contagious disease. We have seen that the islands of the Forth were used for this purpose at an early date. Quarantine implies 40 days from the French word "quarante" meaning forty. This was the period allowed for those carrying disease to become non-infectious. Simson, whose childhood was spent at the Lazaretto on the Queensferry peninsula (at the West Ness of Inverkeithing Bay) says that in the early 19th century 5 or 6 dismasted hulks were moored in St Margaret's Hope and used for this purpose. The "Dartmouth", a frigate, was the last of these to remain. Sometimes the crews riding quarantine in the hulks landed to plunder vegetables and other edibles. A hulk was also moored at Cruickness but this was soon replaced by a land station established by the Government and used during the 1832 cholera epidemic. The suspected carriers of the disease were kept in complete isolation. Food, water and coals were passed through an outside door, which when locked were obtained by the inmates' opening an inside door. Simson recalls that in 1832 the school children were dismissed on account of the cholera epidemic and remembers his father going about the house with a saucer of vinegar and salt petre, and a red-hot poker. The intention was to fumigate the house by dipping the poker in the saucer's contents. In 1835 the Government sold the lazaretto to an Edinburgh lawyer. In Stephen's time (1921) the outside wall of the enclosure was still standing and two doors were visible "the larger for the admission of goods borne upon hand trucks. In the wall there was also an aperture through which food was passed to the men employed within". The past has a delightful habit of reaching out to the present. Sandra Malcolm while typing this script remarked that as a child in Cruickness she and a friend played at throwing a ball through the hatch in this now demolished building.

Other sea-borne visitors came on pleasure trips or merchant vessels. In the 19th century pleasure steamers ran between Granton and Newhaven downstream and Alloa and Stirling upstream, calling at several intermediate places on the shore including North Queensferry. As a boy, Simson remembers watching the steamers racing each other up-river from his vantage point above the village. Fyffe writing a little later notes "the gay passenger steamer rattling up; the huge merchant man tacking across the Firth, the eerie droon of the Ferry passage boat resounding for miles along the drowsy shore." As for the merchant vessels, Lieutenant Cudlip RN who made an Admiralty survey of the Forth in 1848 had counted as many as 300 of these anchored at the one time in St Margaret's Hope

Brodie gives details of other visitors. To start with there was always a guardship lying off North Queensferry, protecting the Hope. Further off, opposite Port Edgar, the black and white painted hulk of HMS Caledonia would have been visible. The HM guardships were as follows:

1850s	"Pembroke"
1860s	"Trafalgar"
	"Edinburgh"
	"Repulse"
1870s and	"Favourite"
1880s	"Lord Warden"
	"Devastation"
1890s	"Galatea"
	"Edinburgh"
	"Sappho"
	"Niger"

There were also state visits. In 1822 George IV was towed past the village in the royal yacht, "Royal George" on his way back from a visit to Hopetoun House. There we are told the sovereign "ate sparingly of turtle soup and drank three glasses of wine". He could do so in confidence because preparations for his embarkation at Port Edgar were in the capable hands of Captain James Scott, Ferrymaster and Superintendent of the passage. The royal squadron consisted of:

Royal Sovereign	yacht
Royal George	His Majesty's yacht
Calliope)	
Cameleon)	Brigs of war

We are told the royal barge "cleared the waves with the velocity of an arrow", and a piper struck up on the Royal George to welcome the King aboard but "during this loyal performance the motion of the boat made it necessary for one of the party to support the piper". The royal yacht was towed out by the steam packet "James Watt". The inns of South Queensferry were crowded out and the town "brilliantly illuminated in honour of His Majesty .... The cannon at Broomhall fired during the greater part of the night". An even more spectacular visit was that of the Channel Fleet in 1860. This was composed of wooden vessels and was accompanied by over 40 pleasure steamers plus countless other small craft. The fleet anchored in St Margaret's Hope to remain there for more than a fortnight, the climax of which was a regatta. The fleet departed on 23rd June "a magnificent sight with every inch of canvas stretched before a favouring wind".

An awesome sight of a different order was the object of another clan of visitors: "when the ball mounts in the air at a finely exalted curvature, reaches out to a distant green and lies white and silent waiting your second stroke there comes a sense of quiet cheer, exhilaration and healthiness which few pursuits so delightfully give" (Cunningham). The pursuit, of course, was golf. The Dunfermline golf club first experimented with a course at Halbeath-Crossgates. Then in 1890 a committee visited the Ferryhills. "The weather was delightful .... there was a charm in the views of the winding Forth and the very air seemed to be impregnated with the game". The result of the visit was a lease on part of the Ferryhills and the opening of a nine-hole course later that year. The grazings were let by the club at £70-75, and by 1893, a full 18 hole course was established. In 1897 the club took possession of Cruicks House for the use of a clubhouse and membership rose to 400.

In "Some hints to Players" we are told about the eccentricities of each hole. We find: "In driving from the tee in "The Trap" (10th hole)

GOLF COURSE ON FERRYHILLS

players who delight in a bit of sport, drive right over the cottage immediately in front", and under hazards and penalties we read that "a ball driven in the garden out from "The Trap" means loss of a stroke". - No doubt fun for the golfers, not for residents.

Amusements

Life may have been precarious in the past, but it was certainly not devoid of enjoyment. Indeed the good times must have appeared all the better in contrast with the bad, and in proportion to their greater infrequency, (ordinary people being far less able to afford celebrations then than they are today). Brock remarks that in the 19th century Christmas was recognised only as a Catholic Festival. The traditional holiday was the second Monday of the New Year known as "Old Hansel Monday". Festive fare included currant loaf, "kebbucks" of cheese and "marrots" stuffed with mashed potatoes and baked. Children made the rounds at Hogmanay with rhymes such as:

"Rise up guid wife and shake your feathers
Dinna think that we are beggars
For we are bairns come oot to play
Rise up and gies our hogmanay"

or

"My feets cauld my shoons thin
Gies me cakes and let me rin"

Simson recalls that at Lammas fair the local herds were turned out on a particularly lush meadow so that they would not need attention and could have their "Lammas Bite". The name was also given to the land used for this purpose. At Lammas there were stalls in Inverkeithing selling gingerbread known as a "Fairin". He won 6d from his teacher for being top of the class. Out of this he gave a penny to the girl he sat next to, spent 3 half pennies riding in the heats of the Lammas fair horse race and the rest at the fair. This was the fair that the 19th century historian, Barbieri said was attended by "masterful beggars, pretended fools and such like vagabonds". He mentions an Act of Parliament of 1449 "by which their ears were nailed to the Tron or to a tree, then cut off and they themselves banished the country to which if they returned again they were immediately hanged. The revival of a single instance of the Act would secure honesty". Mr Barbieri, besides being a historian was surgeon and chemist to the Earl of Elgin. Had his proposal been adopted it might well have created a demand for his professional services.

By all accounts the Ferry children had a field day at the time of the cattle trysts. These occurred in the autumn, the main ones being at Crieff and Falkirk. Black cattle from the North were driven down the drove roads to these vast open air markets. Relatively few came via North Queensferry but those that did made the ferry a busy place. Here the village boys joined enthusiastically in driving the cattle onto the boats. The sheep presented little dificulty but cows often got detached from the main herd. Some fell off the pier and had to be driven up the beach and back onto the pier again. At this time (All Hallows) the surrounding fields were crowded with sheep and cattle waiting to make the crossing. For this, two boats were used - the half-tide boat which was a single masted sloop with mainsail and jib, and the Don Juan a

mastless hulk with seats all round for conveying passengers. The latter was towed by a tug. Both these vessels lie rotting on the shore of the Inner Bay. Soon, little will be left of them. One of the taunts levelled at the ferry boys by the lads from Inverkeithing was:

"Wha' robbed the drovers?"

Perhaps this refers to some forgotten, but once celebrated act of exploitation. If this were so it would have been some feat, judging by Haldane's description of the drovers who would have given as good as they got.

Simson recalls that one of the sports for local lads was to steal a ride on the back of gentlemen's carriages. Seeing this the other boys would advise the driver to "whip behind". He also remembers the threat: "if you were a brither o' mine I would tie a wisp o' strae about ye and stap ye up the lum". This referred to the custom of putting a bag up the chimney during Summer to stop draughts. In winter however, the bag was taken down for the smoke to get out. Before retiring at night a large piece of coal would be put on the fire, the ashes and cinders were then drawn around its sides. In the morning it would be mostly burned but the cinders were dry and inflammable and could be used as "gathering coal". Brock recalls another taunt directed at Wattie Kiddie who came from Inverkeithing to sell fruit and vegetables:

"A' ye buddies come and see
Wattie Kiddie drinking tea"

While he chased some of them away, the others stole his pears. To a bad baker they called:

"Batchy, batchy bow wow wow
Canna bake a penny row"

The Don Juan 1977, looking N.W.

Stephen explains that during times of famine the Inverkeithing Town Council would purchase food to retail to the people at reasonable prices (just as the North Queensferry Sailor's Society did). A dealer, Charles Coutts, was suspected of exploiting this and from then on his effigy was burned annually, first being carried round the Burgh and then hurled from the Town house onto a fire built at the mercat cross. Brock notes the same custom in the village, on Queen Victoria's birthday saying that the boys dug up a tree stump and dressed it as a guy, carrying it on their shoulders and set fire to it on the beach.

Two of the most charming of Fife sayings (which may well have been current here) are noted by Mackay. The first is a type of incantation used to avoid work. The second needs no explanation

> "Curly doddy do my biddin
> Soop my hoose and shool my middin*"

> (*Midden ie heap of human dung
>   which would be located outside
>   each house)

> "I hae laid a herrin in saut
> Lass gin ye lo'e me.   Tell me noo
> I hae brewed a forpit o' maut
> An I canna come ilka day to woo"

The old people may well have enjoyed "an infusion of agrimony" rather than tea as the New Statistical Account of Inverkeithing suggests. But others required something stronger. It is no coincidence that amongst the old buildings in the village, the two hotels are by far the largest, a testimony to the importance attached locally to drinking. Before 1964 "bona fide" travellers came here to slake their thirst and to avoid the rigours of licensing laws. In the early 19th century there were 13 places in the village "where spirit may be bought in small quantities and drunk upon the premises". Even further back in time (1669) the judge of the Dunfermline Regality Court "considered the desyre and petition of the brewers of the North ferrie making mention that whair they be dischairged for selling of aill above the rait of sexteine pennies of the pynt. They have representit that they will be forced to give up brewing in respect any chainge they have is from gentlemen and strangers that pass at the ferrie who will not drink the aill that they might brew at that pryce. Doe thair for notwithstanding of the sd. act doe dispenss wt the brewing and selling of aill at twentie pennies the pynt the same being sufficient as shall be attestit by Wm Wellwood who is heirby appoyntit cunster". Cunsters were visitors appointed by the various crafts to monitor quality and prices. The magistrates fixed maximum prices for commodities such as candles, malt, ale and bread. Brewers or others selling above these prices would normally be fined by the Court. Obtaining the Regality Court's permission to sell wine at 20 pence per pint had therefore been a wise precaution.

The largest concentration of inns stood conveniently at the pier head. The first, known as the Old Inn or Mrs Malcolm's Inn, was immediately North of the Signal House. Next came a property which we now know as the paper shop. Between this and The Albert Hotel (then the Hope Tavern) was James Cunningham's Inn

established in 1754 and removed 120 years later. On the other side of the Main Street opposite the Albert Hotel was B Drummond, Vintner and on the Brae was a maltbarn, coble and still belonging to Alexander McRitchie, a name associated with the malt trade in the late 17th century. Yet another inn is mentioned in the Dunfermline Guildry records. The site may well have been in Battery Road. The details are as follows. In 1765 the Guildry bought Sebastian Swinton's house and lands on the ferryhill for £200. They proposed to fit it out as a public inn. A vintner John Adie applied to take the tenancy on a 19 year lease paying a rent of 12 guineas per annum. An old house adjacent was also bought for £4 and John Monroe, "mason in Inverkeithing" was employed to undertake the conversion. This included cutting the rock "for an chaise road" and "building a sea-dyke opposite to the new jamb". Several complications ensued. Swinton was reluctant to deliver title to the property; Monroe was behind with his work and Adie failed to deliver to the Guildry the double of the tack, ie his agreement to the tenancy. As far as one can gather, following a successful court case against Swinton who was by now provost of Inverkeithing the Guildry opened its inn. James Cunningham was another of the Guildry's tenants, (besides being innkeeper, tacksman and ferry boat skipper). Here relationships seemed to be easier, for the Guildry authorised their treasurer "to drink a guinea with James Cunningham .... provided he pay and clear up his rent crop for 1779 betwixt now and Whitsunday next".

Before concluding this section reference must be made to the village regattas. These were held every Summer. Rivalry with South Queensferry was keen. North Queensferry produced several fine rowing teams which competed all over Scotland. The team for 1882 was:

> Peter Penny   (Bow)
>
> Peter Syme
>
> Robert Dowie
>
> Robert Syme   (Stroke)
>
> Peter Anderson aged 12-13   (Coxswain)

A newspaper article gives the following details of the 1876 regatta: "The village during the afternoon was exceptionally busy and the principal thoroughfares were crowded with people". The boat races were:

	Prize Money
Pleasure boats not exceeding 20'	£1-5-0
4 oared Jolly boats not exceeding 24'	3-0-0
4 oared Jolly boats not exceeding 18'	1-10-0
2 oared Jolly boats with coxswain	1-0-0
2 oared Gigs not exceeding 24'	1-0-0
4 oared Jolly boats confined to boys under 16	0-12-0

The first of these races was for sailing boats. The course was by the East of Inch Garvie and round "HMS Favourite" the guardship. It was won by D D Blair in "Marmion" in the time of 34 minutes 20 seconds. However, on measuring his boat it was found to be 1½" longer than the regulations allowed. Strenuous objection was made by Mr William Martin who had come third in "Concord". A vitriolic exchange of letters in the local press ensued but was closed by Mr Blair in the following terms: "I have sometimes heard of a class of mortals in this world said to be possessed of half inch souls but I never anticipated coming into contact with such a one so nearly approaching that class, more especially at a regatta".

Brock's description of the village regattas is a verbatim account of an anonymous local contributor. ".... the pier and every spot where a favourable view could be had of the course were crowded with spectators. The fun started on the Friday night with the mooring of the Commodore's boat off the Old Ferry Pier, and also of the turning buoys. The holders of sweetie stalls which lined both sides of the main street claimed their stances ... On the Saturday morning given a favourable wind and dry weather the programme started with a yawl race with one lugsail. There was great excitement when 5 or 6 yawls got away with a "hale sail" breeze. Famous competitors were "Scotia", "Jane and Marion", "The Brothers", "Foam" and "Margaret". But the Derby of the day was the 4 oar jolly boat race". The names of the boats were "Mary Jane", "North Ferry", "Tiger" and "Lizzie". In the later 1880s lighter boats were used such as "Bonnie Dundee", "Ferry Lass", "Try Again" and "Swallow". In 1897 a village rowing club was started opposite the Albert Hotel in the rowing club hall. This was used for dances, socials and concerts. Eighteen foot boats such as "Briar Rose" were kept beneath the premises built as a canteen for the railway bridge construction workers. It is now demolished and the ground used as a children's playpark. World War I put an end to these activities. After the war, however, a new club was formed but "gradually again of recent years a lull in the enthusiasm has set in. There are so many new interests for the young men and the motorbus quickly takes them away to the big centres. Besides a boat of the type now required in competitions is expensive; a 20 ft jolly boat costs about £80 and this with the expense of transporting it is a formidable consideration for a small village. Some five years ago the Rowing Club Hall was once again closed; the club's boat still remains in store but is out of date. In former days practically every family owned a boat and all the children could row and manage sails; now this is far from being the case. For this state of affairs many people blame the railway company as they charge 10/- rent for boats lying on their ground (viz the shore of the two village bays). But this is not the whole explanation .... Counter attractions have much to do with the present eclipse of what ought to be a foremost sport in a seaside place like North Queensferry".

Finally we have the description of one of our oldest residents, Peter Roberts. This is based partly on his father's reminiscences. The main street was lined with stalls selling gingerbread and sugar hearts. The pubs did a record trade. Such was the crush that a lot of the beer was spilt and quite literally ran from the doors. The village boats were "Briar Rose", "White Rose" and "Red Rose". The champions from the West Coast used to black lead the bottom of their boat to get it to run smoothly through the water. The ferry boys would remark "good boat you've got there" and surreptitiously try to rub it off. Other regatta events were a duck chase for swimmers (the ducks had their wings clipped; the object was to catch one); a greasy pole with a flag on the end extending horizontally from the pier over the water (the object was to seize the flag; inevitably contestants fell in the water); a barrel race in which competitors were given a half a barrel and oars (unless the competitors were careful a pull on the oars would set the barrel spinning round and round).

The Roxburgh Hotel. September 1977

POST SCRIPT

The 20th Century

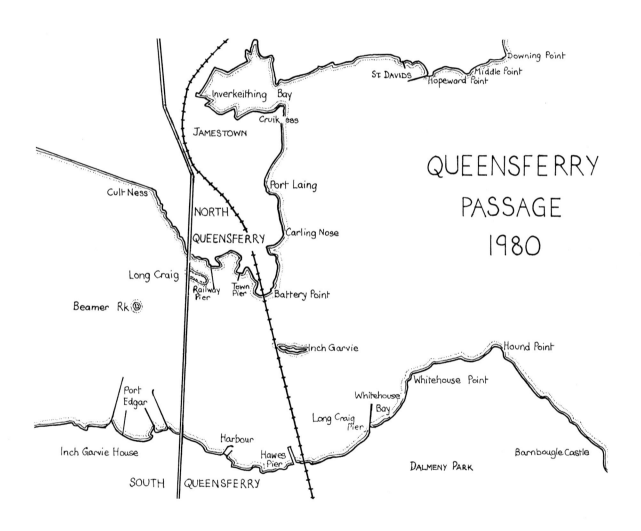

QUEENSFERRY
PASSAGE
1980

Downing Point
Middle Point
St Davids
Hopeward Point
Inverkeithing Bay
Cruik ess
JAMESTOWN
Port Laing
Cult Ness
NORTH
QUEENSFERRY
Carling Nose
Long Craig
Railway Pier
Town Pier
Battery Point
Beamer Rk
Inch Garvie
Hound Point
Whitehouse Point
Port Edgar
Whitehouse Bay
Long Craig Pier
Harbour
Inch Garvie House
Hawes Pier
DALMENY PARK
Barnbougle Castle
SOUTH QUEENSFERRY

The village

To tell the history of North Queensferry in the
20th century would take a book in itself. The
significant changes have been the decline in
local employment, the increase in residential
accommodation, and the gradual increase in
prosperity of the community so that the village,
apart from its spectacular situation, has
become much like other residential areas. Even
before the closure of the ferry, this was

becoming apparent. A writer to the local
newspaper in 1933 complained "but now since the
start of the North Queensferry Development
Association everything is whist drives and
dances". The North Queensferry Development
Association was an association initiated by
Dr A J Brock to improve the amenities and the
recreational and cultural facilities of the
village. Under its auspices a children's
garden was laid out, an annual horticultural
show arranged, allotments opened, the Brae
decorated with flower beds, public seats set out,

and a village institute opened.

Another significant element in the 20th century has been the frequent presence of the military on the Queensferry peninsula. In both world wars the area was fortified and manned. In several places concrete bunkers and gun emplacements remain. Contemporary accounts tell of the posting of sentries between here and Inverkeithing so that residents had to answer in order to pass on their business. In the first world war, observation balloons were housed in giant hangars on the present site of Inchcolm Drive and here a Victory Ball was held in 1918. A submarine depot was planned at Port Laing and biplanes were launched from that beach. Across the water at Port Edgar flying boats were moored. Indeed at the start of the second world war villagers got an even closer look at the military at work when German planes made an attack on the Railway Bridge and on naval vessels moored nearby.

On several occasions the Home fleet arrived. Enormous cruisers and battleships were moored downstream from the Railway Bridge and were therefore familiar sights. Mrs Marjory Sim (nee Webster) recalls "when Carlingnose Barracks was fully manned the Sergeants' Mess personnel arranged dances, and when the fleet was in, their opposite numbers from the warships were invited, along with local young ladies. It was all a very exciting time, (for the young men too) since we were all invited on board ship. On one occasion a party of about 20 had an invitation to tea on board "Nelson". When we had had tea and watched a film show, we found that the last liberty boat for the North side had gone, which meant we were landed at South Queensferry instead. Even the last ferry had gone and there were no trains either. We had to hire a motor boat from the Hawes Pier and we hardly had enough money among us to pay for it. It was a lovely life".

The Passage

Following the opening of the Railway Bridge, some of the animation left the village. Most of the itinerant workers who had worked on the construction now sought work elsewhere. Nevertheless villagers still found employment from the upkeep of the bridge, the continued running of the ferry in compliance with the law, and from an expansion of quarry-working. In the early years of the 20th century, the ferry was a shadow of its former self, supplementing its timetabled runs with sightseeing trips on the Forth. It was administered by a series of lessees, until it returned to the direct control of the North British Railway in 1920. At this stage the old ferries, "Forfarshire", "Woolwich" and "Dundee" worked the passage. The latter could carry 997 passengers but only 10 cars. The ferry was therefore ill-equipped for the age of the motor car. During the 1920's the number of road vehicles using the ferry increased steadily and it became clear that changes would be necessary to accommodate the traffic.

During the economic depression of this period the shipbuilding yard of William Denny and Brothers of Dumbarton was short of work. Sir Maurice Denny approached the LNER (successor to the North British Railway) with a proposal to build two modern car ferries. The LNER made the counter proposal that if Denny provided the ships, the Passage could be leased to his company. The proposal was accepted and thus two new ferries, "Queen Margaret" and "Robert the Bruce" were launched in 1934. Brodie, on whose work this account is based, describes them as follows: "side-loading with a draught to suit the existing piers and a spartan passenger saloon in the after forecastle .... Each paddle was operated independently by a chain drive from an electric motor, and bow and stern rudders were fitted to give maximum manoeuvrability. While "Queen Margaret" had a conventional riveted hull, her

Mary Queen of Scots

sister was the first ship to be entirely electrically welded .... Each vessel cost approximately £22,000 and could carry 28 cars or a maximum deck load of 60 tons. The double ended design dispensed with the time wasting business of turning the ship and with its introduction a regular half hourly service was possible".

high winds, a design was chosen which would prevent a recurrence of the Tacoma Straits tragedy. This suspension bridge literally blew itself to bits. The Forth Road Bridge is designed to swing by as much as 20 feet in the middle, in a 100 mph gale. In addition, open grills between the carriageways allow the wind to blow through the bridge, rather than to lift it from underneath.

STAGES IN THE CONSTRUCTION OF THE FORTH ROAD BRIDGE

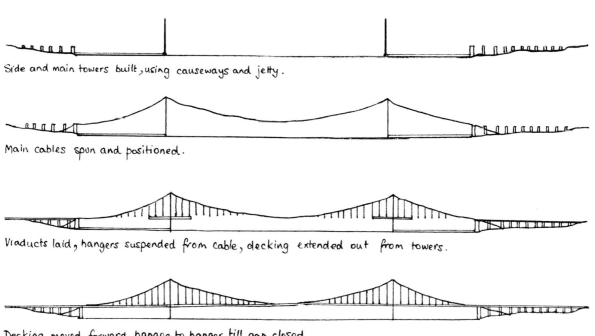

Side and main towers built, using causeways and jetty.

Main cables spun and positioned.

Viaducts laid, hangers suspended from cable, decking extended out from towers.

Decking moved forward hanger to hanger till gap closed.

In 1949, a third ship, "Mary Queen of Scots", almost identical to the two existing vessels was brought into service. Finally in 1955 the larger "Sir William Wallace" was launched and brought into service the following year. From this time until the closing of the ferry in 1964, the ferry was operated by 4 vessels, providing a 15 minute service. It is in this form that many travellers remember the ferry: with its queues of cars on either side, its curious black and white craft crossing the river crabwise, and the brief maritime interlude they afforded to journeys North of Edinburgh. Several employees of Denny's of Dumbarton still live in the village. In the early sixties I remember examining with considerable interest a photo of deckhands of the "Second Snark", a pleasure boat which ran in the Summer months from Queensferry. The photo was of two comely girls wearing white roll neck sweaters bearing the elephant crest of Denny's. One was to be my wife and the other my sister-in-law.

Before the closure of the ferry, it was carrying over two million passengers and 900,000 cars annually, but even this immense effort could not keep abreast with the demands of progress. The project to build a road bridge over the Queensferry had been long-planned and much delayed during the 20th century. Government finally gave its consent to this project in 1958 and preparatory work began. Bearing in mind, the extremes of weather experienced in the area, particularly the

The first phase was to build the piers on which the main towers stand, the subsidiary piers to carry the side arches and to excavate the cable anchorages on either side. These anchorages were built to withstand a pull of 14,000 tons. Each tunnel now contains 10,500 tons of concrete. The main pier on the North side stands on Mackintosh rock. Concrete towers carry the side span onto terra firma. Ferry Barns farm which stood at approximately this position was a casualty of building the bridge.

With the main piers in position, work began on the towers. Each tower consists of two legs joined together by bracing, which rise 512 feet above sea level. The towers, made of steel boxes each 40 feet long, and weighing 30 tons were stacked one above the other. In November 1961 the first four wires of the cables of the bridge were hauled over the top of the towers and anchored on either side. Now began the lengthy process of "spinning" the suspension cables. These are made up of 11,618 parallel high tensile steel wires, each 0.196 inches in diameter. Nine months later the cables were complete and hangers were lowered from them to receive the steel structure on which the carriageway would be built. The steel deck was now extended from either side of each tower. The main span was completed on 20th December 1963 when the steel structure projecting from the two towers was joined in the middle. Computers had forecast a gap of 0.37 inch. In practice it turned out to be only 0.25 inch.

The target date for completing the bridge was 1963. Completion was delayed by about 12 months, primarily due to bad weather. During the final 3 years of construction, 25% of available time was lost as a result of high winds, rain and snow. Indeed the men who erected the towers suffered from vertigo and the equivalent of sea-sickness as a result of the unsupported towers swaying in the wind. The unfortunate Minister of State for Scotland who visited the bridge during construction was stranded for over an hour in an open lift on the main northern tower. A 50 mph gale was blowing and later he was confined to bed with a chill. Those who built the bridge were given special clothing. In addition precautions were taken to reduce the swing of the bridge and to protect the men from accidents; four gigantic safety nets were suspended beneath the structure; the men wore safety helmets and had the use of safety harnesses. Thus compared with the 57 deaths during construction of the railway bridge, there were only 2 deaths resulting from the construction of the bridge itself.

An indicator of the importance of the bridge was the significance which visitors attached to its formal opening. In the first 5 hours from its opening 29,000 vehicles crossed. Thousands of others waited in queues stretching up to 7 miles from the bridge. The toll collectors hands were said to be stiff and bruised from thousands of knocks from non-stop drivers handing over their half crowns.

Another way to comprehend monumental undertakings is via their statistics. For the two bridges at Queensferry we can make the following comparisons:

	Rail Bridge	Road Bridge
Years taken to complete	8	6
Original estimate	£1.6M	£16M
Completion cost	£3.4	£19.5M
Length	8,296 feet	8,259 feet
Steel used in construction	54,160 tons	32,500 tons
Peak labour force	4,600 men	390 men
Maximum height	361 feet	512 feet
Number of workmen killed	57	2
Age of bridge	91 years	17 years

Last, we can look at the new bridge from the point of view of the two Queensferries. Now two bridges, each a miracle of engineering but differing so markedly in design and appearance, stretched out to join these two ancient communities. The needs of national economic development had finally brought to a close the story of the Queensferry passage. Far from being a fusion and junction of the ways however, the new bridge represented a new departure: for from this time onwards the two communities that had been welded for centuries in a single enterprise were parted both from each other and from their origins. Working the passage had been a source of income, and a source of pride. It was therefore with mixed feelings and backward glances that the villagers awaited

the arrival of the Queen for the formal opening of the Bridge and the final closure of the Ferry Passage

The day chosen for opening the bridge was 4th September 1964. Preparations were made for 100,000 spectators and 16,000 invited guests. Unfortunately the weather was poor, with visibility down to 50 feet because of a harr, as a sea fog is called locally. Royal Navy vessels assembling to form a lane of honour for the Queen when she returned by ferry from the North side, and to provide a 21 gun salute, manoeuvred gingerly in the fog; two collided and another glanced off the Beamer rock. At 10.55 am Queen Elizabeth and Prince Philip arrived at Dalmeny the former in "a sapphire blue wool coat with matching shaded hat of gathered tulle"; the latter "wore a grey lounge suit and carried a brown soft hat". The main ceremony occurred on the South side and was followed by a 21 gun salute, and the breaking of flags from the top of the bridge towers. Later a burst of rockets was detonated above the Railway Bridge. Then with the weather improving the Royal party crossed the bridge for a shorter ceremony on the North side. Here a plaque was unveiled with the following inscription:

"Her Majesty the Queen, accompanied by His Royal Highness the Duke of Edinburgh first crossed this bridge on 4th September 1964. The Queensferry Passage was thus superseded after 800 years of continual use"

The Royal party recrossed the river aboard the ferry boat "Queen Margaret" en route for Edinburgh where lunch and a 35 foot replica of the bridge covered in 4,000 multi-coloured dahlias awaited them. This brought to an end the official celebrations.

Two days later a more intimate ceremony commemorated the passing of the old ferry crossing. Five hundred people, mostly from the Queensferries, attended a special service on board the ferry boat "Queen Margaret". The service was conducted by the Rev. Troup of Inverkeithing and North Queensferry who described the last ferry voyage of the "Queen Margaret":

"with the band playing "Auld Lang Syne" and with people waving on the Railway Bridge and yachts surrounding the ship with their crews, and streams of cars on the new Forth Road Bridge, I counted it a great honour to be invited to preach on that occasion, and to give thanks to God for the countless number of great seamen who in days past and very recent days have manned the Queen's Ferry: they that go down to the sea in ships, that do business in great waters, these see the works of the Lord and his wonders".

Bibliography

Balingall, W	The Shores of Fife	Edmonston and Douglas 1872
Barbieri, M	A descriptive and historical gazeteer of the counties of Fife, Kinross and Clackmannan	Maclachlan & Stewart 1857
Bensen, R A	South West Fife and the Scottish Revolution: the presbytery of Dunfermline, 1633-52	M.Litt Thesis Edinburgh University 1978
Beveridge, D	Between the Ochils and the Forth	Wm Blackwood & Sons 1888
Beveridge, E	A bibliography of Dunfermline and the West of Fife	Wm Clark & Son 1901
Blatchley, A T	The passage of the Forth	1960
Brock, A J	Brock papers Series of articles	Manuscript Dunfermline Press October 1932 - January 1934
Brodie, I	Steamers of the Forth	David and Charles 1976
Chalmers, P	Historical and statistical account of Dunfermline	Wm Blackwood & Sons 2 volumes 1844 and 1859
Cunningham, A S (Editor)	Inverkeithing, North Queensferry, Limekilns, Charlestown and the Ferry Hills	Wm Clark & Son 1st Edition 1899 2nd Edition 1903
Dick, S	The pageant of the Forth	T N Foulis 1910
Dickson, J	Emeralds chased in gold: the islands of the Forth	Oliphant, Anderson and Ferrier 1899
Douglas, H	Crossing the Forth	Robert Hale Ltd 1964
Gardner, L	Stage coach to John O' Groats	Hollis and Carter 1961
Haldane, A R B	The drove roads of Scotland	Edinburgh University Press 1952
"	Three centuries of Scottish posts	Edinburgh University Press 1971
Hall, B	An account of the Ferry across the Tay at Dundee	1825 Abertay Historical Society Reprint 1973
Hammond, R	The Forth Bridge and its builders	Eyre and Spottiswoode 1964
Mackay, Ae J G	A history of Fife and Kinross	Wm Blackwood and Sons 1896
Mackay, T	The life of Sir John Fowler	John Murray 1900

Mason, J	The story of the Water Passage at Queensferry	Wm Denny & Brothers Ltd 1962
Millar, A H	Fife pictorial and historical	A Westwood & Son 1895
Nicholson, F J	Sketch of an old school house	Scottish Educational Journal September 1937
Phillips, P	The Forth Bridge in its various stages of construction	R Grant and Sons 1889
Prebble, J	The high girders	Secker and Warburg 1956
Purvis, R	Sir William Arrol	Wm Blackwood & Sons 1913
Sibbald, R	History of Fife and Kinross	1710 Reprinted Cupar, Fife 1803
Simson, J	Reminiscences of childhood at Inverkeithing or life at a lazaretto	1882
Sinclair, J	The Statistical Account of Scotland	Wm Creech Edinburgh 1791
Stephen, W	History of Inverkeithing and Rosyth	G & W Fraser 1921
"	The Story of Inverkeithing and Rosyth	Moray Press 1938
Webster, J M and Duncan, A A M	Regality of Dunfermline court book 1531-1538	Carnegie Dunfermline Trust 1953
Westhofen, W	The Forth Bridge	Reprinted from "Engineering" 1890
Wilkie, J	The history of Fife from the earliest times to the 19th century	Wm Blackwood & Sons 1924
"	Bygone Fife from Culross to St Andrews	Wm Blackwood & Sons 1931
—	Duncan's itinerary of Scotland	Glasgow 1823
—	Report of the committee appointed by the managing trustees of the Queensferry Passage	1828
—	The banks of the Forth	Jas Lothian 1862
—	The Forth Bridge: a concise account of its history with unique illustrations	Freemans Press Inverkeithing 1947
—	The Forth Road Bridge - the official story	Forth Road Bridge Joint Board 1964
—	Topographical, statistical and historical gazateer of Scotland	2nd volume 1843
—	The new statistical account of Scotland	Wm Blackwood & Sons 1845